BACKPACKING ACROSS NEWFOUNDLAND

AN ILLUSTRATED JOURNEY

A THIRTY DAY TREK THROUGH THE NEWFOUNDLAND INTERIOR FROM WEST TO EAST

GILBERT L. PENNEY

BREAKWATER BOOKS LTD.
100 Water Street
P.O. Box 2188
St. John's, NF
A1C 6E6

Canadian Cataloguing in Publication Data

Penney, Gilbert.

Backpacking across Newfoundland

ISBN 1-55081-151-7

1. Newfoundland–Description and travel
2. Backpacking–Newfoundland
3. Penney, Gilbert–Journeys–Newfoundland.
4. Penney, Gilbert–Journeys–Diaries. I. Title.

FC2167.5.P45 1999   917.1804'4   C99–950039-2
F1122.P45 1999

Editor: Shannon M. Lewis
Design/Layout: Jonathan Holden
Printed in Canada

Copyright © 1999 Gilbert L. Penney

Canada We acknowledge the financial support of the Government of Canada through the Book Publishing Industry Development Program (BPIDP) for our publishing activities.

TABLE OF CONTENTS

I dedicate this book to our wives, Gleason and Barbara, without whose support and patience our treks would not be possible.

Our Route

A map of Newfoundland showing the route with the following labeled locations: St. Anthony, Gros Morne National Park, Corner Brook, Robinsons, The Grasses, Annieopsquotch Mountains, Granite Lake, Maelpaeg Reservoir, Bay d'Espoir, Pipers Hole, Terra Nova National Park, Sunnyside, St. John's

I.   GETTING THERE

Atop a craggy ledge slightly more than halfway to the crest of a steep mountain gully, Harvey Rice and I pause briefly to refill our aching lungs. My legs are wobbly, my breath comes in short gasps, and my heart pumps wildly against my chest.

For the past thirty minutes—or was it thirty hours?—we have tediously inched our way up the narrow gully, following a 'path' carved by a tiny brook that tumbles merrily down the mountainside. We have carefully negotiated slippery black rocks and hoisted ourselves upward by clinging onto overhanging branches. At times we have even crawled on hands and knees, laden by our heavy packs, through narrow openings in the thick brush that crowds the stream.

It is near noon on a chilly, partly cloudy July day in 1995. Since leaving camp at seven thirty a.m. we have been engaged in a massive struggle to lug ourselves and our sixty-pound backpacks around Mica Pond. This, we decided yesterday after carefully studying the country and the map, was the best way to get to this gully and the high country beyond. Once on top of the mountain we know we will be *really* on our way.

There is no denying it now. My legs, lungs, and heart scream the news. Our long-awaited and meticulously-planned trek from Robinsons on Newfoundland's west coast to Sunnyside more than five hundred kilometers to the east has officially begun.

With packs propped beside us and our boots tucked firmly beneath our backsides for that extra bit of purchase, we gaze westward from our lofty position. At a glance we can view the country over which we have traveled these past two days. Directly beneath, ringed almost entirely by dark, brooding mountains, sits Mica Pond. It lies at the end of a hilly gravel road that winds along the north side of the beautiful Robinsons River valley. Our eyes easily trace the river gorge, its edges gently rounded by a carpet of dark green forest, as it snakes its way sea-ward.

It is there, where Robinsons River empties into the waters of Bay St.George, that Harvey and I, resplendent in brand new hiking gear, first lifted our new Gregory packs, grasped our Leki hiking poles, and posed for a few departing pictures. As the camera's unblinking eye stared coldly at me I had tried manfully to assume a casual, relaxed stance beneath the unfamiliar weight of my Volkswagen-sized pack. In my mind's eye I can even now picture myself in the slightly bent posture, my hiking pole planted firmly among the beach rocks for extra support. What should have been a confident smile was instead a painful grimace.

After the pictures were snapped, and a few parting pleasantries exchanged with our photographer and driver, Rick LeDrew, we set off at eight thirty a.m. for yet another 'trip of a lifetime'—a walk across Newfoundland.

Gilbert Penney (left) and Harvey Rice (right) standing on a beach at Robinsons on Nfld's west coast ready to begin the trek to Sunnyside.

DAY 1

The weather is warm but partly cloudy as we climb up the sandy embankment near the beach and begin to walk along the narrow gravel road that takes us to the paved streets of Robinsons. Neat picket fences on both sides of the road carve the grassy rolling pastureland into irregular blocks occupied by quaint homes and summer cottages. The air is fresh and clean, and a lone man watches curiously as we trot along, striving to settle into a rhythmic gait. Our loads are not yet comfortable, and we have not yet picked up the rhythm that will later become automatic as we measure each step of the long journey with the plant and lift of our hiking poles.

In an hour we graduate from gravel road to paved street. Walking briskly now, and with surprisingly few rests, we leave Robinsons behind and head for the Trans Canada Highway, about seven kilometers away. A sudden shower had forced us to scramble into the thick bushes that hug the edge of the pavement. Waiting for the cloudburst to end, Harvey checks his feet for the first time . So far, so good.

By ten thirty we reach the TCH, where just east of the Robinsons' turnoff we stop at a roadside restaurant for a cold Pepsi and a bowl of soup. We especially savor the cold drink since we know the memory of it must linger until we reach the Burgeo Highway several days' trekking to the east.

We do not enjoy the walk along the highway shoulder from the restaurant to the beginning of the gravel road that will take us to Mica Pond. The weather has now become hot and it seems the entire distance is a gradual, exhausting climb. The continuous whoosh of cars, trucks, and tractor trailers is an unwanted distraction. Already we are anxious to leave this noisy pandemonium and begin hiking in the peaceful solitude of the wilderness.

Thankfully, with a slight westerly breeze there are no flies, and we carry our weight well. By early afternoon we reach a small wooden bridge where we stop for a long rest, soaking our feet in the chilly water and enjoying a light snack.

We spend the remainder of the afternoon hiking a further eight kilometers along a gravel surface that is punishing to our as yet uninitiated feet. Harvey's feet, despite his earlier fears, are holding up very well. Mine, however, are a different matter. I had decided to wear two pairs of socks rather than the usual single pair and am now paying the price. My feet feel as if they are clamped in a vise, and on the downhill the toes scream in pain. For me, the glorious hike quickly becomes nothing more than a test of my pain threshold.

Later that evening, after hobbling into a small clearing about a hundred meters from a tiny brook, I help Harvey set up our tent. Before supper Harvey tries to catch one of the microscopic trout we had seen in a small pool beneath the bridge. The trout live to see another day.

Day 2

This Sunday we awake to a drizzling rain. It had poured overnight, but there are signs this morning that the weather will soon clear. Sure enough, by eight thirty the rain stops. After completing the first of what is to become a breakfast routine of cereal and pancakes, we have our tent down, our gear packed, and are ready to head for Mica Pond, some eighteen kilometers distant.

Before leaving, Harvey doctors a blister on my left foot. This is a new experience for me because on all of our previous trips it had been Harvey's feet that required constant tender loving care. Although he demonstrates great concern, I am convinced that Harvey is secretly pleased the blisters were now 'on the other foot.'

Not one of our typical campsites (near Mica Pond). The tent has been blown over by a gust of wind

This morning we both experience the agony of pulling stiff, damp boots onto sore feet and fitting heavy packs on tender shoulders and hips. Our hips are, in fact, rubbed an angry red where the stiffly padded belts of the packs had made chafing contact the previous day. Although pleased about their carrying capacity, we are as yet doubtful about the comfort level of these expensive new packs. As for me, I have so much soreness at this stage that the night before I was convinced I had overloaded myself. Harvey and I discuss the situation and agree that wherever possible I will lighten my load. The cold light of morning, however, quickly shows that to actually discard any of the items we had so carefully packed is not an easy matter.

With the rain over, the day turns out to be excellent for hiking. A chilly westerly wind and a heavy overcast sky keep both sweat and flies at bay. At noon when we pause for a delicious, stomach-filling meal of macaroni and cheese, we have already travelled eight kilometers. Only ten more to Mica Pond.

We spend the remainder of the afternoon doing some hard hiking, despite the fact that we are still on a paved road. As we steadily rise from the shore-level of Bay St. George, most of the going is uphill. We have been travelling constantly through thickly wooded country which falls off rapidly to the right into the valley of the Robinsons River. Occasional glimpses of the river and the brooding dark faces of the mountains where we are heading provide scenic diversions during this stretch of otherwise monotonous walking. Also, about three kilometers from Mica Pond we look down onto the dark surface of Black Gulch Pond. It is nestled deep and sheltered beneath the towering forested mountains to the south and west. A beautiful secluded spot. In many ways, this entire valley reminds me of the several days we had spent along the north side of Lloyd's River during our trek across Newfoundland from south to northeast two summers earlier. River valleys, I thought, provide their own natural beauty.

And we are confident that plenty of scenery lies ahead.

My left foot has by now become a source of excruciating pain. The blister is okay, but I had banged my foot against one of those huge rocks that pimpled the road and jammed an already tender big toe. When we reach Mica Pond at four thirty p.m. and spend another half an hour searching for the easiest route to the high country tomorrow, I am relieved to finally ease my tender feet out of my boots and slip them into a pair of comfortable camping sandals.

That evening after eating Magic Pantry beef stew supplemented with mashed potato, and chasing an empty tent as it scudded before a gust of wind, we relax over open maps studying the hilly country that surrounded us on all sides. With thirty-nine kilometers of road hiking behind us, we know that tomorrow will be a different day.

DAY 3

We are up at six and enjoy breakfast in the orange glow of a brilliant sun as it peeks above the high mountain to the east of Mica Pond—the mountain we will tackle today. Despite the early morning promise when we leave camp the sun disappears and is replaced by a grey sky and a chilly wind.

For the first half an hour or so we follow a crude trail along the western edge of the pond. It takes us through patches of tangled trees, along sections of narrow rocky beach, and across small, wet bogs. To avoid slippery rocks at the water's edge and to skirt the knee-deep pits of black mud into which the bogs are torn, we have to do some fancy stepping. We fall in love with our hiking poles as we use them to check the depth of mud and to maintain balance as we teeter, top-heavy, on rocks.

Soon the trail disappears. For about a kilometer we bushwhack through thick mature forest that extends down the steep mountainside right to the water's edge. Fallen trees and huge rocks make progress painfully slow. Taking turns in the lead, we crash and stumble our way towards the long southern inlet from which a small brook flows from Mica Pond to Robinsons River. Here the land is low and hard, with a dense covering of high gowithy, or

Looking at 'The Grasses' east of Mica Pond. This piece of privately owned wilderness has a colourful history.

shrubs. A short detour to a high point gives us a view of 'The Grasses,' an area prominently featured in the lore of Western Newfoundland.

The Grasses is a beautiful, privately owned piece of Newfoundland wilderness. It is an area of tall grass—higher than a man—that looks like a splash of pastel green against the much darker greens and blacks of the shadowy mountains that tower on both sides. Legend has it that early Scottish settlers brought sheep from Bay St. George to this very spot by way of the Robinsons River valley. How they could have done this is beyond me, but after the struggle we had just experienced following a road along the side of this valley, I could only admire their tenacity. Dark stories are also told of murders and suicides that are said to have occurred here.

Standing atop the small knob, staring out at The Grasses, I try to imagine the harsh bleating of a herd of sheep and the ugly violence that once intruded upon its solitude and serenity. Happily nature had, in this instance at least, healed herself.

But the high country awaits. There is still the challenge of the gully. Getting to it proves to be no Sunday afternoon stroll. From the opposite side of Mica Brook to the base of the gully stretches a band of the dreaded tuckamore. We had experienced this before on the Northern Peninsula, in the Long Range Mountains, and on top of the Annieopsquotch Mountains. Tuck is the bane of all hikers who venture into the wilderness of Newfoundland. It is a mass of stunted, deformed conifers that present to the hiker an almost impenetrable wall of roots, twisted trunks, and needle-sharp branches. For a hiker with a sixty-pound load on his back, it is an especially formidable foe.

Motivated mostly by our hatred of it, Harvey and I tackle this band of tuck with a vengeance. We prise apart stubborn, gouging branches and squeeze through narrow openings, careful all the time not to rip out our eyes or—Heaven forbid!—tear our new packs. At times we literally crawl over the tops of the low, matted trees. With an investment of sweat and desperate struggle, and with numerous rests for gulps of Gatorade, we finally reach the gully.

II. TO SANDY POND

And now, here we are, sitting on a ledge, looking back at where we had been. As our hearts resume their normal rhythm, and energy flows back into our legs, we congratulate ourselves on what we have accomplished so far. Already, only three days into our cross-island trek, we have experienced some of the pleasures and endured many of the pains of wilderness backpacking. Refreshed now, we help each other with our packs and begin the final leg of the upward climb. It will take us to a tiny pond on the edge of open country, where we will have a late lunch before heading east toward more pleasures and pains, and eventually the Burgeo Highway.

Here at the top of the mountain the vegetation and terrain are in stark contrast to what they had been at the base. Thick, old-growth forest has given way to rocky, barren country and scattered bands of low tuck. Some areas, especially along the edges of brooks and ponds, are wet and boggy. It is a landscape very similar to that at the top of the Annieopsquotch Mountains, where two summers earlier we spent three difficult days laboriously picking our way eastward.

The map says that we must now travel generally east for about seven kilometers before descending again to the low country. The best route, it seems, is to head almost directly east for about three kilometers, turn to the northeast for nearly two, and then go east again until we reach Sandy Pond, a large pond nestled at the base of the mountain and surrounded by rolling, open country. According to the map, this line of travel is most likely to be free of trees and tuck, and it will lead us directly to what appears to be an open path down to the edge of Sandy Pond.

We spend the remainder of this day as we had spent the morning: doing some strenuous hiking. We inch our way slowly eastward, descending over and over again into narrow valleys and gullies only to climb laboriously up the opposite side. Frequently we stop to remove our packs and rest just long enough to allow energy to flow back into our legs. Often to avoid impassable ponds, cliff faces, and thick tuck, we must switch back and travel away from the direction we want. Progress is slow and painstaking.

The mountain top is broad and, except from high points, no obvious landmarks are visible. We know that an easterly course will eventually get us down off the mountain, but aware of the danger of dropping down into the thick forest on both sides of Robinsons River as it bends around the base of Bumbly Mountain a short distance to the south, we are anxious to hit the open path to which I referred earlier. This means our travel now is largely by map and compass, and the margin for error is small. It is well past six o'clock in the evening when, hungry and thoroughly exhausted, Harvey and I reach the far eastern edge of the mountain and look down upon the placid surface of Sandy Pond and the scenic panorama that stretches off into the distance.

On the right, as if guarding the entrance to the beautiful green open country beyond, is the magnificent Bumbly Mountain. Like a balding, middle-aged man, its top is bare and embarrassingly exposed, its base ringed by a band of dense forest. Far to the east, blued by distance, Sam Butt's Hill, Little Rocky Ridge, and Blanchard's Hill rise prominently above the landscape. Caribou Pond, Three Island Pond, and Portage Lake, as well as numerous other unnamed bodies of water, appear as patches of deep blue against the rich green background.

As always, Harvey and I are awed by the spectacle of mountains, ridges, and lakes emerging from the abstract lines of a map and becoming real, solid masses on a landscape we are viewing for the first time. Once again we are reminded that no map—and even no picture—can truly capture the magnificence of a wilderness scene.

Blanchard's Hill attracts our attention more than the others. That is because on a direct line between it and us looms another hill, forested and over 1700 meters high. The map gives it no name, but from earlier contact with west coast wildlife officials we have learned that on its crest is a wildlife cabin—good information to have in case of an emergency. Not planning an emergency and thus having no intention of visiting the cabin, we nevertheless study the hill carefully. At its base is a large pond which lies directly on the route we plan to take. It is reassuring to see that the country from Sandy Pond to this one should at least afford excellent walking tomorrow.

But tomorrow is another day. The hour is late, and we are still tired and hungry. We must find a suitable campsite before dark. Taking one last appreciative look at the expansive wilderness scene spread before us, we reload our packs and concentrate on the very practical problem of getting down to the shore of Sandy Pond.

The band of white shown on the map and toward which we have been heading all day is now directly below us. We expect, as the map seemed to promise, that it would provide a clear, easy path down to Sandy Pond at the point where Robinsons River empties out of it and begins its journey westward. But no. One glance puts that hope to rest. Instead the entire side of the mountain is covered by old growth forest, much of it dead wood. Very discouraging, especially this late in the day. But it must be conquered and at least, we console ourselves, it will be all downhill from here.

Selecting a point where we believe Robinsons River will be easiest to cross, we set off towards it, descending at a rapid pace. To our delight, the trees prove to be more widely spaced than expected, and scattered among them are enormous ferns the size of small trees. Though fragile in appearance, I think, those monstrous ferns are nature's stubborn claim to beauty amid the harsh ugliness of dead trees and tangled tuck.

Fortunate enough to discover a well-travelled caribou path, we break out after less than an hour on the north side of Robinsons River. It is shallow and rocky, and its banks are tree-covered to the edge. No camping spot here. Anxious now, Harvey and I separate, searching for a place no matter how tiny to set up the tent. After much scouring of the river bank, we finally choose a small area, bumpy and covered with gowithy, on a small point of land formed where the river gathers its water supply from Sandy Pond.

Though not a comfortable campsite, it is scenic. Our tent is set up a meter or two from the river and several meters from the shore of the pond. At its far end we can see some neat, red-painted buildings and a couple of small boats pulled up on the sandy beach. One building, larger than the others, appears to be the main office, cookhouse, or even bunkhouse, while the others seem to be guest cabins. An outfitter's setup, we guess. On the opposite side, almost directly across from our campsite where a narrow band of trees extends to the shoreline, is a small dock from which a series of steps extends up from the shore into the trees.

Harvey and I take turns studying the area through binoculars and are convinced it is unoccupied. Fortunately the proximity of those man-made structures fails to intrude upon the tranquillity of the wilderness setting in which we enjoy our late supper.

It is eight o'clock in the evening and a long, rigorous day of hiking is behind us. Mica Pond is now twelve kilometers to the west, as the crow flies. But we have not travelled as the crow flies. With the climbing and circuitous route-finding, we know we have covered much more distance than that.

And we also know that, unlike the proverbial crow, we have walked firmly on the ground rather than flown over it. Our feet tell us that. I still have some aches and swelling in my left big toe, and Harvey has developed a minor blister on one foot. Enough to make the act of pulling off hiking boots and easing tired, aching feet into airy, comfortable sandals a most exquisite pleasure.

Despite the foot complaints, we are already rounding into shape. Walking through bog and climbing steep hillsides with a heavy pack is quickly doing what practice

Campsite at Sandy Pond, where Robinsons River begins its westward journey to St. George's Bay.

walks back in Springdale had largely failed to do: working the kinks out of our middle-aged bodies.

Our late supper devoured and a quick cleanup completed, we retire directly to our sleeping bags, twisting and turning in classic canine fashion for the most comfortable position between bumps.

That done to our satisfaction, we take stock of the day. We agree that wildlife has been scarce so far. Even though the network of well-travelled trails suggest a heavy caribou population, we have as yet seen very few. Other than two moose, a lone duck, and a bird's nest complete with four or five tiny eggs built in the moss at the root of a tree, wildlife sightings have been a disappointment.

But tonight the gentle lapping of waves against the shore of the pond and the busy gurgle of river water running by our tent lull us to sleep. Wildlife may be less than expected, but this life in the wild has not.

III.   PRINCESS LAKE

DAY 4

This morning we are up at 6:45, well-rested and anxious to begin our fourth day. A gentle southeast wind lends welcome respite from the black flies and mosquitoes that had pestered us during supper last night. A family of five loons watches curiously from just offshore as we gulp our cereal and wash down our usual helping of three small, dry pancakes.

For the first eight or ten kilometers today we know that travelling will be easy. The view from the mountain yesterday had convinced us of that. And the map seems to promise similar conditions at least as far as Rocky Pond, on the other side of Lloyd's River and about fifteen kilometers to the southeast.

At 8:15 we bid fond farewell to beautiful Sandy Pond and its family of loons and begin a leisurely hike along a treeless, gently rolling landscape that resembles an endless pasture. It reminds us of the lovely green pastureland of the Buchans Plateau in the island's interior.

The day being clear and reference points easily visible, we have the luxury of travelling in a fairly straight line without need of a compass. Thus we maintain a steady pace, pausing only to take brief rests and to soak up the delicious wide-open atmosphere. As far as our eyes can see, even aided by binoculars, are low, green hills and ridges interspersed with dozens of small ponds and bog-holes and widely scattered patches of tuckamore. Caribou trails lead in all directions, and caribou themselves are in greater abundance.

By noon we have reached the large pond at the foot of the mountain on which the wildlife cabin is located. In a small cove we relax over lunch.

Just over two kilometers later, after crossing some very wet bog, we ford the upper reaches of Lloyd's River, a river which at this point is really not much more than a large brook. The remainder of the day sees us pass through a broad valley in which is a series of long, narrow ponds. We stay on the north side of these ponds and skirt along the base of Blanchard's Hill. With Rocky Pond now in sight but too far to reach today, we search once again for a suitable campsite.

Like yesterday, one is hard to find. In fact, we hike a short distance up a valley heading northeast, away from our planned route, before settling on a spot of gowithy at the end of a small, shallow pond surrounded by huge boulders. Near our site, a stream disappears beneath the boulders as it heads down the valley.

This evening with our tent pitched among stunted trees several meters from the edge of the pond, we have supper under a grey, overcast sky and feel a definite nip in the air. Taking stock of our location, we see that we are at the base of a low ridge running west to east for about two kilometers before descending again just north of Rocky Pond. Its surface is devoid of trees but enormous boulders are strewn everywhere. Despite the boulders and the ridge's almost moonscape appearance, hiking it should be no problem tomorrow.

As for today, we feel we have accomplished much. The hiking has been great, and we have kept a steady pace, covering sixteen kilometers since leaving Sandy Pond this morning. From one vantage point this afternoon we had been able to spot through binoculars the Annieopsquotch Mountains far to the east, on the opposite side of the

Burgeo Highway, and had even been able to see the shack at the base of the communications tower located on the western edge of the mountain range. Although still quite distant, the sight of these landmarks was reassuring. It meant we were making definite progress towards the end of the first leg of our long journey—the Burgeo Highway.

Day 5

This morning at six we awake to the sound of a heavy, wind-driven rain pounding against our tent. By 8:30, although it is still raining lightly and a gale force southerly wind is sweeping up the valley, we crawl out of the tent, pack our gear, and leave camp without breakfast. Wait for more comfortable conditions to eat, we figure.

Some fog sits upon the ridge, partly obscuring it behind a ghostly veil as we follow a compass bearing across its top. Our destination is a series of small ponds in the valley north of Rocky Pond, two kilometers away. Atop the ridge the ground is hard and rocky, and we are totally exposed to the strong gusts that try to force us backward.

The wind and rain soon dissipates the fog, and we are able to see Rocky Pond a short distance to the southeast. Looking at the pond, it strikes us as strange that this large body of water appears to be much higher than the surrounding ponds and that it does not seem to be fed by any large stream. Only a single small brook flows out of its eastern side, running into the ponds in the valley that we walked through yesterday. Curious that water flows out while none appears to flow in. The pond is sheltered on the southwest by a high, steep ridge, heavily forested. Near the shore is an outfitter's camp that, according to Harvey (who I find to be a veritable storehouse of trivia

Harvey following a caribou path along the banks of Lloyd's River's upper reaches.

such as this), belongs to the Lundrigans. A marvelous setting, I think to myself, for an outfitter.

Once off the ridge we seek out the shelter of an old-growth forest near the edge of a small pond and deep in the woods among the moss and twisted roots have our long-awaited breakfast. It is now 10:30 and in spite of our rainclothes we are both soaked to the skin and in much discomfort.

The remainder of the morning sees us hiking in improving weather towards the spot where we will cross Lloyd's River. The landscape and vegetation are changing. Rather than the rocky, barren terrain of the ridge, the countryside is now thinly forested with fragile looking, pale green junipers. These delicate young junipers and the soft carpet of ground-hugging plant life make our approach to Lloyd's River seem like a stroll in the park.

By noon we have reached Lloyd's River at a point where it bends sharply north towards King George IV

Lake. Broad and rocky, it flows sinuously through the flat countryside, its banks a broad swath of tall, rich grasses rippling seductively in the wind. Well-defined caribou paths dent the grass, paralleling the river. A short distance upstream in an even wider section is a broad, flat island of grass, a pale green splash against the darker shade of scrubby spruce.

Harvey and I pause for awhile and take pictures. But we know full well that no camera—and indeed no words—can capture the unspoiled beauty of this pastoral scene.

Just when we are convinced our eyes have had their fill of pleasure, we are treated to the visual delights of the opposite side of Lloyd's River. Some more comfortable hiking over hard ground, with only occasional boggy interruptions, takes us to the crest of a ridge that affords a magnificent view of Princess Lake. And a princess of a lake it is.

Princess Lake is long and narrow, running generally north to south. Its middle is almost squeezed into two equal parts by opposing points of land jutting out into the lake and approaching to within a hundred meters of each other. While Harvey leans against his pack and studies the far ridges through binoculars, I hike down to the point on our side of the lake just to see how narrow the channel between the two really is. I discover a well-worn caribou trail that leads to the point and ends at the water's edge to emerge again on the opposite side. The intervening channel, though narrow, appears deep and turbulent. Swimming across here, I think, must be a daunting challenge for a young caribou.

In a few minutes, following a lone caribou part of the way, I hike back to the top of the ridge.

We end the day camped in deep woods near the edge of a brook that flows out of the upper end of Princess Lake. Unable to locate a better site, we set up the tent on a tiny mossy area wedged between two trees with just enough room to spread our sleeping bags between the bumps.

Although the sky is still overcast and the air chilly, it is good to be sheltered from the wind. With wet garments and felts from our soddened boots spread on branches to catch the breeze as it blows off Princess Lake, we take a much-needed, invigorating bath in the cold water of the brook. Then for supper we eat the last of our supply of Magic Pantry meals.

Never mind the cold dampness, we are contented hikers as this day ends. Today we have feasted on astounding scenic vistas and walked past small groups of caribou at home in their natural habitat. For what more—apart from a good night's sleep—could a backpacker ask?

Preparing a noonday lunch on a rainy day near Lloyd's River.

IV.   STRIKING THE BURGEO ROAD

DAY 6

The sky is grey with fog when we peek outside at 6:30 in the morning of Thursday, July 20th. But as we eat breakfast the sun breaks through, shining on the rocks in the brook, giving the promise of a good day.

The three or four kilometers from this brook to an old skidder trail proves to be tough slogging. It takes us about two and a half hours to bushwhack to the top of the ridge on the opposite side of the brook and to pick our way across wet bogs and around long, narrow bog holes filled with disgusting black water before finally reaching an old cut over. It is with immense relief that at mid-morning we hit the western end of the abandoned logging road that eventually takes us to the Burgeo Highway just north of Peter Strides Pond, where at a gravel pit trailer site a fresh food supply awaits.

By now the weather has become hot and, after a quick lunch of noodles near a small brook, we exchange hiking pants for walking shorts, ready for a leisurely stroll out the road. We plan to camp tonight about seven kilometers this side of Peter Strides and tomorrow pick up our first food cache from a small storage shed behind a trailer owned by Fred Randall of Burgeo.

Soon we are able to look down upon the southerly finger of the three-fingered King George IV Lake. Here where Lloyd's River enters the lake are several large flat islands of grass similar to the one we had seen yesterday. On the island closest to us we count more than twenty caribou grazing contentedly, totally unaware of intruders. As we watch and admire, an occasional caribou casually splashes across a shallow, sandy-bottomed stream in search of even tastier fodder.

It is a picture of idyllic tranquillity. Despite the buzz of insects and chirping of birds in the heat of this mid-summer's day, a peacefulness and timelessness transcends all activity. Standing on a mound of gravel near the edge of the rocky woods road, I feel like a latter-day Moses looking upon a land flowing with milk and honey.

But this Moses, too, cannot enter the promised land. He must move on. Reluctantly Harvey and I re-shoulder our packs, much lighter now, and continue our journey.

The remainder of the day is a familiar repetition of walk and short rest, walk and short rest. The road takes us along the side of a heavily timbered ridge that runs the entire distance to the Burgeo Highway. Apart from a narrow, unnamed pond about two kilometers in length and the much larger boot-shaped Woods Lake, there are no significant landmarks or features to interrupt the boring

Caribou on sandbar near point where Lloyd's River meets western end of King George IV Lake, an ecological reserve.

sameness of the ten kilometer hike to the highway.

A couple of incidents do, however, help in some small way to relieve the monotony.

You will recall that upon hitting this woods road we had changed into short pants. Harvey had attached his hiking pants to the outside of his pack in order to air them out as we walked—yes, they did need airing out! After pausing at one of the many small brooks that tumble off the ridge, Harvey discovers his pants are no longer attached to his pack. Now those are no ordinary trousers. They are $60 one hundred per cent cotton hiking pants with a pocket for everything except the kitchen sink. They are the ultimate in hiking comfort, and they are a gift from his wife Barb. Harvey is fully aware that he can not proceed without them, and we have no idea how far back the trail they are.

We pow-wow to weigh the pros and cons. Does Harvey go back alone? If so, how far should he go? It is already late in the afternoon: will he get back in time to set up camp? Will it rain while he is gone? Already the sky has grown ominously dark and a shower appears likely. Should we set up camp right here?

After some discussion, the decision is made. I will remain to look after both packs while Harvey hikes back as far as it takes to find his pants. He sets off at a brisk pace, his demeanour that of a man with a mission...and what greater mission can there be than a frantic search for one's trousers?

Meanwhile, with a sheet of plastic and several stripped alders I set about constructing a crude shelter in the bushes at the side of the road, a shelter just large enough to accommodate myself and two packs.

No sooner have I maneuvered my body comfortably around the packs and have settled in for a long wait than

Harvey appears, his pants held triumphantly aloft. The crisis of the missing trousers has reached a happy conclusion.

Shortly afterward, during another of our brief pauses to remove our packs and lay them on the road at our feet I glance at my watch, and it isn't there. No watch! Where could it be? Obviously it has to be somewhere between here and our last stop. My guess is that when I hoisted my pack after our last rest the watch must have hooked in the strap and been dislodged from my arm.

This time Harvey waits while I retrace my steps, searching the ground for my missing timepiece. I find nothing. Disheartened, I turn back with the sad news. After a short time of commiseration, we help each other with our packs—and lo and behold! there it is: the watch lying innocently on my pack. It had been there all along. We had lost time alright, but not the watch.

And this day is not yet over. Having planned to camp about seven kilometers this side of the Burgeo Highway, we spend the reminder of the afternoon looking for a suitable campsite along the route. The idea is to find a reasonably level spot near a brook. But there is nothing. No level spot, no brook. Consequently, nearing exhaustion, we end up hiking the entire distance to Peter Strides. It is seven o'clock in the evening when we locate the key to Fred Randall's trailer and thankfully enter his luxurious accommodation.

Before supper we call home to inform our wives that we have reached the highway and the end of the first leg. Although it has been only six days, it is good to talk to my wife Gleason and to know that back home all is well.

With that comfortable feeling of reassurance we begin to prepare supper in the gathering darkness. Tonight we are to partake of our first freeze-dried meal, one of twenty such meals we will have before the trip is over. Not accustomed to preparing this type of dish and being by nature a meticulously cautious man, Harvey is especially careful to follow the instructions at the back of the water-proof package. Into the pot of rapidly boiling water he tosses the entire contents of noodles, vegetables, and various spices. There remains a tiny envelope of black powder. He asks me what it is for, but for once I don't know. We both figure it must be some kind of flavouring. Harvey peels off the top and pours the powder into the mixture. Immediately our precious meal turns an ugly unappetizing grey. So it was not a flavouring! Careful reading reveals the harsh truth. Emblazoned across the envelope in bold upper case letters are the words **DO NOT EAT!**

Thus ends our initial foray into the delights of the freeze-dried meal. For tonight we must content ourselves by munching on snack foods, but nineteen other freeze-dried delicacies remain for future titillation of our taste buds.

Tonight unable to drift quickly off to sleep in the stuffiness of the small trailer, we discuss our situation now that six days of our anticipated thirty-one-day trek are completed. Physically, we are still suffering from a variety of aches and pains. Although my early foot problems have disappeared, Harvey does have some concerns about blisters developing on his feet. My left hip, mildly arthritic, has been bothering me occasionally at night, and Harvey's left knee has come perilously close to giving out on a couple of occasions. Then there are the pains in the neck that we both endure for awhile each evening after removing our packs—and I do not refer to each other. I refer to the painful stiffness caused by the abnormal position in which we must hold our heads while walking. On the positive side, we both agree that our stamina is improving. After a long day of strenuous hiking we are usually fresh and ready to go the next morning.

As for food, we are eating well. The hours of careful planning are paying off in that our diet is much more varied and satisfying than that we had during the 1993 trip from Burgeo to Halls Bay. Barb's trail mix, a wonderful snack on which to munch during rests, and the Gatorade provided by the Gatorade representative in Springdale are both proving to be worthy additions to our larder. Thanks to this evening's fiasco with our first freeze-dried meal, we cannot yet reach any conclusion as to the benefits or otherwise of this addition to our menu.

Our gear, of excellent quality for this trip, is already proving to be worth its cost. Hiking pants, which we are trying for the first time, are vastly superior to our usual denim jeans. They are lightweight, comfortable, fast-drying and, according to Harvey, easy to lose. Wide-brimmed cotton hats also, besides improving our appearance, have turned out to be much better for hiking than peaked baseball caps. They are fine protection from the sun and great in rain.

Perhaps the most beneficial addition to our gear has been our hiking poles. Not having used them before, they were a somewhat clumsy companion at first. But the poles have become an extension of ourselves, and now we dare not step out onto the trail without them. They help set a steady pace, provide support when footing is unstable, help test softness and depth of bogholes, and serve as a third leg when fording rivers and streams. Without them we feel we would hardly have a leg to walk on.

We could go on talking about the pros and cons, the disappointments and pleasant surprises, the joys and pains of our trip, but night is passing. Comfortable in the knowledge that the first leg is complete, we finally drift off to sleep. The close confines of the poorly vented trailer and the occasional tractor trailer growing to a crescendo of noise before fading into a distant high-pitched whine as it hurtles down the lonely Burgeo Highway makes this a fitful sleep. Already we long for fresh breezes circulating through open tent flaps and the restful gurgle of a nearby stream. Tomorrow night, perhaps.

Looking north from ridge at lower end of Spruce Pond, east of Burgeo Highway. The peaks in the distance are on the south side of the Victoria Lake Reservoir.

V. IT NEVER RAINS BUT IT POURS

DAY 7

After enduring a sweaty night, it is almost a relief to greet a new day. The heavy rain that had pounded off the trailer roof at night has still not completely ended, but there are signs of clearing.

When we finally set off, under full packs now, to hike the eleven kilometers south along the Burgeo Highway to the point where we will leave the road and head across country almost due east, the weather has improved immensely. It is partly cloudy with a brisk southerly wind and, on those occasions when the sun breaks through, hot.

This morning's hike is boring, interrupted only by the novelty of passing vehicles and by a relaxing lunch beneath the bridge at Spruce Brook. We camped here one rainy night on our previous trek when winds were high and the brook angry and swollen. Now the weather is marvelous and the waters of Spruce Brook timid.

It is with some relief that we finally arrive at the point where we are to leave the highway. Here the highway crosses between two tiny ponds—or bogholes. About two kilometers to the east is a high, forested ridge. Between it and ourselves stretches an expanse of soft, wet bog dotted with small bodies of water. We select a line of travel which will take us around the low northern edge of this ridge, and carefully pick our way across the bog.

Having walked on hard surface for most of the past two days, we find the going very difficult here. It is the type of hiking we have endured so many times before, most especially when crossing the boggy country between Buchans and the Gaff Topsails in 1993. Bogwalking with a fully loaded backpack on a hot, sultry day has to be one of the most strenuous of activities. It drains the energy from the legs and causes the muscles to scream with pain as they choke on lactic acid.

Fortunately it is only an hour or so before we begin to climb onto the harder ground of the ridge and navigate through its sparse tree cover towards a long, shallow pond running north to south for about two and a half kilometers. On the eastern side of this pond rises a barren ridge, reaching a height we estimate to be about a hundred meters. At least, we think, there will be good hiking tomorrow.

Following a well-worn caribou path, we walk along the edge of the pond for just over a kilometer to its southern extremity, where a rocky brook flows into it. Here we camp on a beautiful grassy spot right at the water's edge and, while flailing to fend off enormous biting stouts, devour a meal of bottled moose and mashed potato. (The bottled moose was one of the extra treats we had stowed in the five gallon tubs at our food stash back at Peter Strides.)

Tonight, as Harvey tries for a trout from a nearby rock, we sing the praises of our Asolo boots. Despite hiking through wet bog for most of the day, our feet are bone dry. Now if only I could pass so positive a remark on Harvey's continued attempts to land food of the fishy kind!

DAY 8

This morning, Saturday, July 26th, we are up at six and ready to leave camp by 7:45, a schedule that will become routine for the remainder of the trip. Fog partially obscures the ridge to the east, but our spirits are buoyed by streaks of morning sunshine breaking through.

Pampering those aching feet.

From our campsite at the south end of the pond to another large pond near the crest of the ridge is a distance of more than two kilometers, climbing nearly all the way. We are only several hundred yards up the side of this ridge when the promise of good weather comes literally crashing down upon us. A severe thunderstorm breaks violently loose from a heavy black cloud that suddenly and without warning appeared from the west. Jagged lightning splits the sky and sharp claps of thunder shake the earth. Nature is having a rock concert, and here we are at center stage. Harvey fumbles feverishly in his pack for the sheet of plastic that I had used as a makeshift shelter two days before.

Just in time, he retrieves it. Huddled close beneath the plastic, embracing our packs, we are pounded by a deluge from the heavens. Cold rain, driven before a wind suddenly emboldened by the storm's ferocity, bounces off our fragile shelter, soaking the ground. A damp chill seeps slowly into our bones.

I remind Harvey how uncannily similar this is to the sudden cloudburst that had forced us to scramble for shelter beneath another sheet of plastic halfway up the side of the Annieopsquotch Mountains two years before. Now we are once again experiencing the sense of utter loneliness and total helplessness that enveloped us on that occasion.

Gradually the storm's intensity abates. The rain eases to a steady drizzle, the thunder becomes more distant and muffled, and the stabs of lightning grow less frequent. Resigned to the inevitability of a good soaking, we crawl stiffly out from beneath the wet plastic, stash it on the outside of Harvey's pack, and continue towards a monstrous rocky peak that marks the apex of the ridge.

For the remainder of the morning we experience a remarkable phenomenon. The western sky is pure blue, washed clean by the recent storm, while directly above us is the edge of a black cloud that stretches off to the east. Out of it drops a steady drizzle of cold rain from which there is no escape. Despite pack covers, rain clothes, and waterproof boots, we are soon drenched and heavy with water.

As we approach the barren peak and skirt a large pond the quality of the terrain begins to deteriorate. Now we encounter patches of the dreaded tuckamore, and a heavy fog makes it difficult to maneuver around them. Furthermore, caribou trails are scarce and all too often we must crash, stumble, and fall through masses of tangled trunks and roots.

Around noon the sky finally clears and a pleasantly warm sun begins to draw the cold dampness out of our bones.

But now there are other problems.

The heat is humid and sticky. Stouts, enormous and

Prominent un-named landmark between Burgeo Highway and White Bear River. This peak was visible several days before we reached it.

lusting after sweet flesh, converge in threatening hordes to ravish Harvey. Comfortable now, and unmolested, I watch his anguish with some sympathy.

Now as we slowly pick our way southward towards the bottom end of Spruce Pond, which stretches many kilometers to the north, we are nearing a landmark that we had spotted at least three days before while far to the west of the Burgeo Highway. It is a magnificent granite outcropping that stands prominent and aloof above the surrounding landscape. Its eastern flank rises gradually and is covered with low, scrubby spruce. The western edge drops off as a sheer cliff face of ancient rock carved by eons of frost and rain into a mass of giant building blocks. We wonder why this natural wonder stands here, so alone, when three of its cousins, almost identical, dominate the otherwise flat plateau of the Gaff Topsails far to the north. Here it appears alien, a geological anomaly, a freak of nature.

Freak or not, it is solidly real, and directly in our path. Around its base is a band of thick forest that at the outer edge degenerates into a bastion of tuck. It all appears impenetrable.

But penetrate we must. Despite near exhaustion, we push towards a tiny stream that begins near the base of the cliff and descends to a shallow pond in a valley formed by this and the next ridge. We follow this stream as it tumbles over black, slippery rocks, occasionally disappearing underneath the ground—the brook, not us—to emerge again farther down the ridge. Although it is now a mostly clear day, this route takes us deep into the forest where it is cool and dark.

Finally we have reached the pond, skirted around its north end, and are climbing the opposite ridge, following a narrow corridor of relatively clear country to its top. We can now look back at the giant mountain as it slowly but surely recedes to the west.

The panorama that stretches behind us as we ascend this ridge and look back from whence we have come is no doubt awe-inspiring in its grandeur. But to Harvey and myself this is ugly country, perhaps not to fly over, but certainly to walk through, and we are glad to leave it behind. Our preference has been and still is barren country with low, rolling ridges and shallow valleys. And towards the east we can see unfolding exactly that.

It seems that already a full day has passed since this morning's thunderstorm, yet it is only mid-afternoon when we emerge from a band of woods and wade across a shallow stream that flows into the south end of Spruce Pond.

Attacking the tuck on the lower part of the opposite ridge, we begin the ascent towards what we are convinced will be better walking. The enormous expanse of Spruce

Pond now unfolds, stretching northward into the bluish haze of distance. There is a breeze up here on the ridge, and flies are no longer a problem. Hiking has become a pleasure again at last.

At five o'clock, totally drained of energy, we locate a grassy spot at the edge of a small, clear brook and set up camp. Despite the disappointment of having to discard our last meal of beef stew which had spoiled, we enjoy a hearty supper and follow it up with an invigorating bath in the cold stream. It is a fine end to a hard day of hiking through unforgiving country, the type of day that lingers in ones memory not for the pleasure it bestows but rather for the pain it inflicts.

Tonight, after covering fifteen hard kilometers, I have a sore right ankle. Harvey suffers from a pain in his right hip and on both feet blisters which have soaked apart in wet boots. But today we also spotted a family of six ducks, saw a loon in flight, and shivered in fear over the fresh signs of, as Harvey would say, a 'breezely bruin' in the deep woods a short distance back. The bear's deep claw marks in a fallen log were a vivid reminder that we would be wise not to surprise this baby in the forest!

But why worry? After all, we *are* a full day closer to Sunnyside.

VI.   WHITE BEAR RIVER

DAY 9

Today is Sunday, and a beautiful Sunday it is. A warm southerly breeze caresses the ridge's spine as we walk along it, heading northeast to White Bear River. This ridge, barren and mostly dry with only scattered patches of tuck and spongy bog, offers excellent hiking. We believe today will be a leisurely stroll to the river, where we will spend a restful night. But things don't always unfold as expected!

White Bear River is one of several that lie between us and Sunnyside which are cause for some concern. Last summer when we travelled to the Granite Lake area to investigate the feasibility of various sections of our route we had tried to learn as much as possible about this river. On the map it is shown as very broad, flowing through a deep, forested valley almost directly southward from White Bear Lake, a large lake fed by Burnt Pond River from the north. A visit with the men stationed at the Hydro site on Burnt Dam promised us that it could be crossed, but we could never be sure.

Both Harvey and I are filled with anticipation and perhaps a little trepidation as we set out this morning. What if the advice we had been given turns out to be wrong and we are unable to cross? It would not be the first time we had been given incorrect or incomplete information. What if we are forced to backtrack and head north in order to cross at Burnt Dam? The going would be difficult, we knew, and we would be set back by several days. Perhaps our food supply would not even last that long.

Clearly the thought of being unable to cross White Bear River is not pleasant to dwell on. I, for one, push it out of my mind and concentrate on the present.

The scene spread before us this morning is both expansive and beautiful. On our left, stretching far to the north, is Spruce Pond. It is an enormous body of water which feeds into Burnt Pond and eventually via man-made canals into the Granite Lake-Meelpaeg reservoir system. Now its surface is an azure blue glistening with patches of sparkling silver as it reflects the slanted rays of the morning sun.

To the east and south is magnificent barren country with blue ridges lined up one behind the other, hiding what we know are large bodies of water, numerous expanses of bog, and thousands of bogholes—all of it untouched and unspoiled wilderness.

To the northeast, our route for today, the immediate prospect looks good. The ridges are higher and drier; and so long as we choose our course astutely to avoid several large sections of forest, we appear to be in for a leisurely day of Sunday hiking.

And until late afternoon a leisurely day it is. We have just climbed to the top of the last high ridge between us and White Bear River, which is now only three kilometers away. Our compass bearing has been set to take us to a clear path through heavy forest on the north and south sides of the ridge. From here we just might get a glimpse of the river and thus have some early idea as to how wide it really is.

From our vantage point atop the ridge we survey the new country that has just been opened to view. And there, less than three kilometers away, glistening in the late afternoon sun, is a long narrow body of water. It appears to be directly across our route, and it looks to be very wide and very deep. Can it be? No, it can't be the river!

We take turns studying it through binoculars, and there seems to be no doubt. It sure looks like White Bear River. And our worst fears appear to have been confirmed. Surely this is impassable!

At this point, in the rush of adrenaline, we make our first real error since the trip began. Without studying the situation any further to determine that we are indeed looking at a section of White Bear River, we set out on a tear for the beckoning body of water. We must know, and the sooner the better.

In record time we reach the water's edge and discover both to our chagrin and relief that we have been needlessly rushing headlong towards a long, narrow pond, not a river at all. In fact, we find that a fast stream flows out of the north end of this pond and runs into White Bear River.

It is nearly six o'clock and, despite our plans of an easy day, we are already bone tired. The river is still over four kilometers away, farther distant than it had been almost two hours ago.

Grimly, we backtrack along the edge of the pond and angle down the side of a long ridge that will take us into the deep valley through which the river flows. Not until we have walked for some time in the cool evening air of an ancient forest do we finally reach the river bank. And there it is. A wide river, alright, but shallow, and strewn with enormous boulders.

We cross easily, using our hiking poles for support as we go from rock to rock, reaching the opposite shore near a small, wet, grassy area. Without even bothering to search for a better site, we set up the tent, have a late supper, and immediately retire for the night at eight thirty.

A day that began as a perfect backpacking day has turned into an ordeal. Rather than enjoying a scenic, relaxing hike across ridge tops and concluding the day with an early evening camped near a beautiful river, we have suffered through a long, trying journey covering twenty-four kilometers, many of which were unnecessary.

White Bear River, though magnificent, still does not impress either of us as one we may want to visit often.

VII. ON TO GRANITE DYKE

DAY 10

Our campsite on the east bank of White Bear River is at the bottom edge of an immense forested ridge which rises gradually to a flat, boggy crest and then descends to the shore of Granite Lake seven kilometers away. A little used gravel road runs along the south side of Granite Lake, beginning at Granite Dam at the western end of the Granite Lake reservoir, crossing over Granite Dyke on the south, and continuing on to Granite Canal at the eastern extremity. The road is one section of a much longer gravel access that begins at Millertown in Central Newfoundland and runs south and east, eventually ending at the Victoria Control Structure on the south side of Victoria Lake. It is a long, hard road, rocky and unyielding to a hiker's feet.

It is to this road we are headed today.

This morning as we leave camp it is wet and foggy, and black flies accompany us in pesky clouds. The fog is low and dense, obscuring our vision and lending trees at the edges of small clearings an eerie, ghostly appearance. Distance and size are deceiving. The only reality on which to rely now is the map.

Taking careful compass bearings, we navigate through wet trees, soaking ourselves to the skin, hopping from one boggy clearing to another. Slowly we climb the ridge, fighting all the while against the uncanny urge to angle to the right, a mistake which would find us entangled in the thick scrub on the ridge's south side.

Soon a steady drizzle has set in. The caribou trails—which we are happy to follow whenever we find them heading where we want to go—are quickly becoming linear masses of black, oozing mud tightly gripping our boots, releasing them with a protesting sucking noise against the insistent tug of leg muscles. Conditions are miserable now as, cold and totally uncomfortable, we trudge through the soft terrain up a steady incline which is draining us of every ounce of energy.

Eventually nearing the top, we reach a stand of mature forest which provides a measure of protection from the drizzle but raises some concerns as to whether, despite our caution, we have indeed drifted too far to the right. Consulting the map we see a band of green with the thin blue line of a brook running southward smack dab through the center. This, we guess, is our present location.

To confirm it, Harvey scouts ahead for some distance while I stay behind to guard the packs. For a few moments, too miserable to sit on the mossy, wet tree skeletons lying in tangled profusion about the forest floor, I stand alone in the midst of a remote silence broken only

Harvey preparing evening meal of our usual fare: freeze-dried food.

by the loud rhythmic splat, splat, splat of enormous rain-drops falling from the branches of trees high above.

In all of history, I muse to myself, how many humans have stood alone on this spot in this remote little patch of forest? Chance are, none. The thought fills me with an eerie sense of intrusion, similar, I suppose, to the twinge of guilt one would feel when entering forbidden, private land. Rather than feeling at one with this place, I feel more like an intruder and am anxious to get out of here.

Soon Harvey returns with the good news. There is indeed a brook, exactly where the map says it should be.

So now at least we know where we are. And despite the fog, we are right on target.

Without further ado, we take an accurate bearing to a narrow passage between two small ponds which lie about a kilometer to the north at the very edge of the ridge. We continue to the edge of the high timber, crawl with great difficulty through a thin band of shoulder high tuck, and follow a careful course across the ridge-top bog. In less than half an hour we hit the narrow passage dead on. After the uncertainty of a six-kilometer walk over featureless terrain in thick fog, it is a relief to realize that finally only a downhill jaunt of a kilometer or two lies between us and the Granite Lake road.

The tiny isthmus between the two ponds proves to be nothing more than a mass of very deep mud with here and there a tuft of sod or a scattered rock which might serve as stepping stones to the opposite side. To test the depth of the mud I thrust my hiking pole in as far as the grip and still find no bottom. Neither of us is anxious to sink into this marshy morass.

It is perhaps less than ten meters to solid ground on the opposite side yet we plot our course very carefully before attempting to cross. Every strategically placed stone and piece of sod is considered and, if possible, tested for stability. Finally, with Harvey in the lead, we tiptoe gingerly across, careful all the time not to linger on any piece of footing that under the combined weight of sodden bodies and packs would disappear into the mud.

It is now only a matter of following a narrow stretch of bog down the side of the ridge. Less than half a kilometer down we encounter an unexpected bonus: an all-terrain vehicle trail runs along the side of the bog and cuts through the woods, taking us over firmer ground. The ATV trail, obviously a popular route for hunters heading to the top of the ridge, leads directly to a large gravel pit about a kilometer to the west of where we had intended to hit the gravel road. Although a bit farther west than we would have preferred, we accept the convenience of such good travelling with profuse thanks to whoever had the foresight to put it there for us.

Although still two days away from our next food cache and a scheduled meeting with Jack Rice, Harvey's father, and Jim Huxter, Harvey's father-in-law, we both feel a major sense of accomplishment at this point. The road in a sense tells us that for all intents and purposes we have completed the section of our trip from the Burgeo Highway to Granite Lake.

But today is not yet over. In fact it is only lunchtime. A short distance from where the gravel pit road meets the Granite Lake road we stop near a small brook to eat a hasty, uncomfortable lunch. The drizzle that was steady all day has now become a torrential downpour. Huddled in the ditch at the side of the road beneath our sheet of plastic, we manage to prepare hot noodles and tea—a meal that today is intended not for gourmet pleasure but merely sustenance.

As if the discomfort of the noontime meal is not enough to test my normally very positive outlook on life, I am shocked at this point to discover that I have a missing fork. Now that may not seem to be a major disaster to the reader. But consider this: this particular fork is a vital one-third of a 'nesting' cutlery set that had already accompanied me for nineteen days from Burgeo to Halls Bay and had served me well on numerous camping trips and day hikes since then. Forkless, the knife and spoon have no companion with which to nest. More significant, perhaps, than its emotional attachment, the missing fork was intended to serve an important function during this trip. It was to enable me to partake of our usual freeze-dried main meal. A spoon simply could not, as they say, "cut it." What implications could this have for the remainder of the trip? Would it have to be called off for the sake of a lost fork?

Harvey tries to console me: "Maybe Dad or Jim will have an extra fork," he says reassuringly. But I know full well they would never think to bring an extra fork. Why would they? Besides, even if they did, it would likely not nest with my remaining spoon and knife.

Despite Harvey's valiant attempt to console me, I must confess here that for some time afterward on seeing him using his fork with great relish I would harbour some resentment against him. The picture of what happened is even today clear in my memory. Just prior to leaving camp at White Bear River the day before Harvey and I had been cleaning our breakfast dishes at the river's edge. His responsibility had included washing the cutlery, which involved, of course, nesting it as well. I am convinced he did not and carelessly left it on the rocks near the river. Perhaps some day, with the passage of time, I will find it in my heart to forgive Harvey.

But back to the present. Curled beneath the plastic, rubbing wet shoulders with the cause of my grief, I spoon hot noodle soup into my body in a futile effort to drown my sorrow.

The four kilometer walk that takes us from here to Granite Dyke is a march through a monsoon. Rainsuits and wide brimmed hats simply cannot repel the sheets of rain that lash at us from the east. Even our waterproof pack covers are unable to provide adequate protection for the contents inside.

How pleased we are that during an exploratory trip to this area last summer we discovered a comfortable hunter's camp near a small brook at the base of Granite Dyke. We had thought at the time that this camp, owned by Clarence Andrews and Wayne Morgan of Carbonear and left open to visitors, could serve as a welcome hostel during our cross-island trip.

Now our goal is to get as far as Granite Dyke and into the dry confines of this camp.

We reach it at two in the afternoon. The tiny brook that last summer had trickled less than two meters from the door has become an angry stream rushing with abandon into the valley that eventually by way of White Bear River will take it all the way to the south coast.

We pick our way around the swollen stream and enter the camp. Thankful for the supply of dry wood inside, we soon have a roaring fire blazing in the heavy, cast iron stove and every single one of our garments hanging from nails, beams, and nylon rope strung from corner to corner. The heat from the stove and steam rising from wet clothes turn the little cabin into a virtual sauna. But with the door wide open, and stripped to our shorts, we enjoy an evening of relaxation reading old copies of the *Evening Telegram* that had been left lying around since last fall and analyzing reports crudely scribbled on the walls and ceiling of the exploits of numerous hunting parties that had occupied the camp before us. After the rigours of the past few days since leaving the Burgeo Highway, tonight is luxurious, surpassing even the luxury of the proverbial five-star hotel.

VIII. THE GRANITE LAKE ROAD

DAY 11

Today, Tuesday, July 25th, is a scorcher right from the start. Even as we leave camp just before eight the air is hot and stifling. Although without a thermometer, we are convinced that by mid-afternoon, as we maintain a steady but sweaty pace along the south side of the gigantic Granite Lake Reservoir, the temperature is at least in the low thirties.

Aware that we need to reach the Granite Canal by tomorrow evening, we plod painfully on through the heat of the day. The combination of heat and hard, rocky ground causes the soles of the feet to burn like fire and at every tiny stream we stop to remove our boots and socks to soak throbbing feet in the cold water.

The scenery is no longer a pleasant diversion. There is nothing to relieve the monotony of hills and turns as the road unfolds endlessly before us. At times we plod for long distances, neither of us speaking a word, each lost in his own private world with only the sharp, repetitive clacking of carbide hiking pole tips marking off the distance.

At one point the monotony of the day is broken by the arrival of a pickup truck approaching from behind in low gear, twisting and turning to avoid huge rocks protruding above the road's surface. In the truck are two men. Curious at the sight of two scruffy bearded men, obviously middle-aged, struggling along under heavy backpacks in this desolate part of the world, they stop and inquire. We tell them who we are—two school teachers from Springdale—and what we are trying to do—become the first people to walk across Newfoundland from west to

Resting on Granite Lake road during rainy day.

east as well as from south to north. For awhile we're not sure as to whether they are impressed or amused.

Then they introduce themselves. They are both from Bay d'Espoir and are stationed at the Hydro site on Burnt Dam about twenty punishing kilometers back. They are en route to Pudops Dam some hours to the east at the base of the Maelpaeg Reservoir to check the water level and will be returning later in the day.

The pickup continues on, bouncing crazily out of sight, while Harvey and I watch with envy, wondering what it would be like to ride rather than walk. They will reach the end of Granite Canal in a couple of hours at the most; we cannot expect to get there until late tomorrow. Oh well, in this backpacking business one has to accept the good and the bad.

The bad continues until late afternoon when we reach Pinsents Pond 18.5 kilometers from last night's comfortable lodgings at Granite Dyke. We have an early supper and relax for a couple of hours, delaying setting up the tent on the level spot we have chosen close to the road. Our hope is that if the tent is not set up when the Burnt Dam guys return from Pudops they will offer us a ride with them to Burnt Dam where we will spend yet another luxurious night in the splendour of the hydro station situated there.

The evening hours pass quickly as a couple of curious caribou lingering close by keep us entertained and we take turns fantasizing about the sensual and gourmet delights that await us tonight at Burnt Dam.

But these delights are not to be. Our tent has been set up, and darkness has nearly set in when the pickup finally slides to a stop before an expectant pair of hikers.

No, they won't be coming back this way tomorrow, they state. But would we like to have some of their food? Would we?! Of course we would! A couple of fruit cups, a tin of sausages, a box of purity crackers, and a litre of Gatorade are passed to eager hands through the open window.

As our effusive thanks fade behind them, the two angels of mercy disappear into the gathering darkness.

Thus we get our second supper.

Tonight is cold and clear, with no hint of a moon. Perfect conditions for stargazing. Harvey, an avid watcher of the night sky, pulls out his July charts and coaxes me out of the cozy warmth of my sleeping bag to share his excitement.

Reluctantly dressing and crawling out into the chilly night air, I look to the heavens and am awestruck by the black, diamond-studded canopy that stretches from the edges of a wild and barren earth. Back home in the dazzle of street lights the sky is usually non-existent. There people go about their nightly activities totally unaware of the grandeur and majesty above them. Here tonight with not a single man-made light to interfere, the sky has become palpable and real. I sense I can reach out and touch it. It is closer, pulsating with life. Stars twinkle brightly, tiny pin-pricks of light move steadily and purposefully in predetermined paths across the blackness.

Standing there, craning my neck upward and straining my eyes to distinguish constellations that Harvey insists are as plain as the nose on my face, I experience some weird sensations. At one moment, with the sky touching the horizon and stars seemingly a short distance above my head, I feel like a giant, a Colossus astride the earth. The next moment I feel I have shrunken and become a mere speck in the vastness of the universe that stretches up and out.

With the infinite patience of a good teacher, Harvey helps his shivering, half-interested student distinguish Cassiopeia, Arcturus, Vega, and the fascinating 'teapot' from among the millions of twinkling lights, all of which seem to be clamouring for equal attention.

Lesson ended, we retire again to the cozy confines of our tent, where our attention shifts from contemplation of the stars to considerations of a more earthly nature. It is a serious discussion about a possible change to the route we had planned to follow from Granite Lake to Bay d'Espoir, seven or eight days to the east.

Last summer during our exploratory visit to this area we had decided that from Granite Lake our course would be across the upper reaches of Grey River, over Wolf Mountain, along the east side of Wolf Lake, around the south end of Dolland's Pond, and northeast from there across West Salmon River to connect with a gravel road leading to Bay d'Espoir.

Now we are questioning the wisdom of this plan. Based on our experiences to this point, we have learned not to depend entirely on the map when it comes to vegetation. Although most of the area in question shows as white on the map, and therefore barren, in reality such is quite likely not the case. In fact, last summer during a side trip to Grey River we had already discovered that the valleys could be forested and the sides of ridges infested by tuck. Then we had to consider the likelihood—or inevitability—of fog as we headed so far south. The fog itself would not normally present a major obstacle to travel, except that fog in combination with tuck could be a real p oblem. If, as we feared, the going would be so difficult as to force us to go back, we knew the trip would have to be cancelled because there would be nobody to meet us at Granite Lake with extra supplies. Finally, there was the problem of communications. Our rented radio-telephone had so far proven to be virtually useless, in that we could rarely make contact with the outside world when we really needed to. With only two of us in the party, what if one should become incapacitated and unable to travel? What could the other do?

Considering these and other factors, we begin to talk about the pros and cons of walking instead northward along the eastern side of the giant Meelpeag Reservoir, crossing Noel Paul's Brook, Ebbegumbeag Dam, and West Salmon Dan just southeast of Cold Spring Pond, from where we could connect with the same gravel road leading to Bay d'Espoir.

The disadvantages of this route were obvious. It would require several days of road walking—never an appealing mode of travel—and we had no maps for the area. The advantages would be the assurance that no major obstacles would lie in the way and the greater likelihood of communication with our families in the event of an emergency to us or them.

Having at least conceded that the Ebbegumbeag route would improve our chances of eventually reaching Sunnyside and the successful completion of our dream, we agree to delay the final decision until tomorrow. After all, we still need the maps, and more importantly, what will Jim and Jack think of the idea?

We talk long into the night. Even after our conversation has petered out, sleep is evasive. Harvey in particular is still greatly concerned about the ramifications of such a significant departure from our planned route, and I sense that he lies awake for a long time mulling it over.

Like ourselves, the loons on a small pond to the south seem to be in a state of confusion tonight. Normally their lonely, haunting cries would lend soothing background music to a night camped near a pond. Tonight, however, something strange is happening in the wilderness. The loons are all night long engaged in a frenzied cacophony of weird screams and frightening screeches. Some unknown primal ritual? Whatever the cause, on this night their behaviour reflects our own emotions.

IX. ANGELS OF MERCY

DAY 12

Today under a grey sky and against a chilly wind we set out to hike the remaining distance to Granite Dam. This morning we walk steadily and silently, each still privately weighing the decision which we must soon make.

Occasionally throughout the morning Harvey thinks he hears the approach of a vehicle. Convinced it is the familiar sound of his Toyota Four-Runner arriving with a fresh supply of food and other goodies, he forces a brief pause each time to listen closely. Each time, nothing.

Then around noon, after we have already covered about twelve kilometers, the familiar grey Toyota appears unexpectedly around a bend. Jim Huxter is at the wheel, Jack Rice in the passenger seat, and every other available square inch of space occupied by all of the 'basic' requirements for a two-day camping excursion to Granite Lake.

The vehicle bounces to a stop, the two elderly men climb out for a stretch and a chuckle at our expense, and Jim produces a camera. Not a flattering picture, I'm sure.

With the necessary greetings quickly dispensed, Harvey and I drop our packs and pounce immediately upon the two dozen Pepsi buried in a huge cooler of ice piled atop the luggage at the rear of the Four-Runner. As we gulp the ice-cold liquid and devour a lunch expertly prepared by the two experienced outdoorsmen, we all discuss our proposed course alteration.

They both think it a wise decision and immediately begin to make plans to obtain the necessary maps. Tomorrow they will drive to Grand Falls-Windsor—even to Gander if need be—to purchase the maps and return that same day. Only anyone who has travelled the Granite

Lake road from Millertown can appreciate the commitment such a trip would require. The many hours of bouncing over rocks and potholes would test younger men, much less the aged bodies of those two.

Plans made, and our mental and physical loads lightened somewhat, Harvey and I set out to hike the remaining eleven or so kilometers to the canal while Jim and Jack go on ahead to do some fishing, set up their tent, and begin to prepare the hearty salt beef dinner which they have planned for us.

In only two hours we reach the campsite, a roadside clearing only a few meters away from the raging waters of the canal rushing headlong to an inlet of Meelpeag, less than a kilometer to the east.

It is still only four in the afternoon, and with somebody else to take care of camp chores, Harvey and I enjoy a very relaxing evening. We drive—a luxury after twelve days walking!—along the north side of the man-made canal that runs the six kilometers from Granite Lake to Meelpeag. We explore Pudops Dam and its sluice gates, examining the mechanism that the guys from Burnt Dam operate in order to control the level of water in the reservoir. We bathe in the deep water below the gates and spend the remaining hour before dark searching for Jim and Jack, who have wandered off somewhere in their quest for the ever elusive excellent fishing spot.

Relaxed minds, full stomachs, and the knowledge that tomorrow begins the third leg of our journey induces sound and restful sleep tonight.

DAY 13

Harvey and I leave camp at seven o'clock this morning to begin the thirteenth day of our trek. It is raining hard, and the air is close and humid. Mosquitoes circle in droves, searching for exposed flesh. Fortunately rain jackets and hoods, though warm and stifling, provide some protection—from the flies, that is, not the rain. (We concluded long ago that raingear in this type of weather is to be worn merely as a formality. In less than an hour we are invariably sogged to the skin, raingear or not. Someday, perhaps, we will be able to afford Goretex.)

Today we devote entirely to hiking directly northward along the east side of Meelpeag Lake. Travelling light, we aim to reach as far north as possible before dark so that tomorrow we can be sufficiently advanced to cross Noel Paul's Brook and begin the journey southeast to Ebbegumbeag Dam. We estimate the entire distance should take no longer than four days.

Simultaneous with our leaving camp, Jim and Jack commence their punishing twenty kilometer journey to Millertown and then to points beyond in search of the two

Yet another meal of noodles!

maps we will need for navigation to Cold Spring Pond. On their return, they promise, barbecued steaks, onions, and Pepsi will be our evening fare. Having eaten a jiggs dinner with a spoon the evening before, my fervent prayer today is for a fork to ease consumption of what I know will be a large juicy T-bone at day's end.

Like yesterday, we maintain a torrid pace, especially after the rain ends around mid-morning. The road is long, winding, and hilly with thick forest crowding both sides. Scenery, except for a few brief glimpses of Snowshoe Pond late in the afternoon, is non-existent.

The monotony of the day is broken only by what I believe to be an amazing development in the unfolding saga of the missing fork. At some point, as I am trudging along in my accustomed position several meters behind Harvey and watching the ground for painful protruding rocks, I spot a white plastic fork. I make a brilliant joke to Harvey about coming to a fork in the road. He chuckles politely, and we continue on.

A short while later, however, I see a second fork lying partially hidden in the gravel at my feet. Picking it up, I notice its tines are bent and it looks a trifle dirty. This time I am strongly tempted to keep the fork at least until after tonight's steak dinner. But Harvey, a bit of a 'fuss-budget' when it comes to the danger of consuming bacteria and dying in the wilderness during a hike, offers some discouragement to this idea. I toss the fork away. But a pattern of circumstances is emerging that I believe to be more than just fortuitous.

Sure enough, later that afternoon a third fork miraculously appears on the road before me. Harvey, although walking ahead, does not see it. This fork appears intended for my eyes only. Once again I bend down (and bending down with a pack on ones back is no easy matter, I assure you), I bend down and reverently grasp the eating tool.

This one is a magnificent piece of cutlery. Its four tines are straight and strong; its handle is broad and flat, and engraved with an ornate design. I admire it aloud, and Harvey urges me once gain to throw the 'garbage' away. But should I treat with casual disdain an object of such great import? No way!

I keep the fork. It serves me well for the remainder of the trip, and I still treasure it today.

Apart from The Miracle of the Three Forks, the day is only a hazy memory. Kilometers stretch slowly behind us, and it is late evening before Jack and Jim finally arrive from their journey to the civilized world.

After some painful driving back and forth, squeezed among the luggage in the Four-Runner, we eventually settle on yet another roadside clearing. While Harvey and I set up the two tents, our hosts for this evening barbecue our steaks, mine being rendered even more delicious when balanced at the end of my brand new secondhand fork.

Supper done and dishes washed, we study the maps that the guys had driven all the way to Springdale to procure. Among other things, they tell us to our astonishment that today we have walked a total of 35 kilometers! No wonder our feet are sore!

X.   To Ebbegumbeag Dam

Day 14

After last evening's bone chilling cold, this morning turns out to be pleasantly sunny. It is already hot when Jack and Jim drop us off at the spot where they had picked us up late yesterday.

Bent nearly double now beneath freshly laden packs, we watch with some envy as the Toyota with its comfortable plush seats bounces crazily out of sight. Another long day of road travel lies ahead.

Our plan today is to continue north along the side of Lake Douglas and then pick up the road that is to take us to Noel Paul's Brook. Noel Paul's being another of those streams that we have not previously checked out ourselves, there is as usual some question about the ease with which we will be able to effect a crossing. Once across, we plan to hike only a short distance before setting up an early camp. Small reward, we tell each other, for the strenuous thirty five-kilometer journey of yesterday.

In spite of the heat and the heavy weight of our packs, we make surprisingly rapid progress this morning. In fact, by noon we have already covered the approximately ten kilometers to the branch that will eventually take us to Ebbegumbeag Dam.

Another short distance and we have reached the edge of Noel Paul's Brook. This is a beautiful, fast-moving stream that empties out of the north end of Lake Douglas and follows a long circuitous route through forested country, eventually connecting with the Exploits River and thence the Bay of Exploits. Standing on a large boulder surveying the river, both up and downstream, I can only guess at the unwritten and long-forgotten events that must have unfolded here. As part of the water system that feeds the Exploits, this was once prime Beothuk country. How many healthy young Beothuk, lovers of the wilderness and takers of its bounty, did at one time push their birch bark canoes past this very spot? Could a tribe of Beothuk, perhaps, have camped here? Did the blood of the Beothuk, their flimsy wooden arrows no match for the guns of white men, run red like ochre in this water? I could only wonder.

Today there are obvious signs of civilization. A well-worn road swings to the left of the grassy embankment on which we stand and disappears at the water's edge to emerge again on the opposite side. Obviously a vehicle crossing.

Partially submerged alders along the shore indicate the water is higher and therefore faster than normal at this time of the year. Nevertheless, after taking a few pictures of ourselves with a magnificent cone-shaped mountain upstream serving as a scenic background, we cross without incident.

On the other side we pause for our noonday meal, made more enjoyable this time by four cans of Pepsi shared between us.

Just as we are finishing up, the unexpected arrival of two vehicles—a pickup and a sport utility—forces us to scramble our gear to the side of the road. We watch with fascination as first the pickup and then the sport utility slowly cross the swollen river, angling slightly downstream as they approach our side.

The occupants are as surprised to see us as we were to see them. Curiosity forces both vehicles to a stop at our roadside lunch site and in response to their queries we tell them yes, we are walking, and no thanks, we don't want a ride. Where have we come from? Robinsons. Yes, we are headed to Ebbegumbeag Dam, as they are. But we're going past that, to Sunnyside. Sunnyside? But isn't that out by Bull Arm? Surprise, some skepticism, some admiration.

They are two weekend fishing parties from Little Heart's Ease. We tell them we expect to reach the dam tomorrow. They reply that they expect to be there in an hour or so. Leaving us behind as two specks in the distance, they speed off towards a relaxing weekend of fish, food, and frivolity.

The specks plod doggedly on. Contrary to our plans, we do not stop and set up an early camp now that we are on the eastern side of Noel Paul's Brook. Instead we walk seemingly forever throughout the hot afternoon.

At first the monotony is broken by numerous roadside cabin sites, most of them neat with impeccably groomed lawns and yards. Soon, however, even those novelties peter out and the long, sweltering afternoon blurs into the repetitive pattern that has dogged us since leaving Granite Dyke on Tuesday.

Most of the time only the sharp, metallic click of hiking pole on rock and the scuff of boots on gravel break the silence. Occasionally a lone caribou, surprised by our appearance, stands petrified in the middle of the road, hind legs splayed apart and a jet of urine making a streaming rivulet in the dust, before it collects it wits and prances aimlessly away. Often a family of spruce grouse (of which there is an unbelievable number in this area) emerges with a frantic flutter of wings from the bushes less than a hiking pole's length away and manages clumsy airborne migration to the opposite side of the road.

We walk with the routine that has become imprinted over the past several days. It is a routine that sees us at regular intervals sprawled in the dust at the side of the road, backpacks resting unsteadily against our hiking poles, munching on trail mix and relishing tiny sips of warm but thirst-quenching Gatorade. A routine that forces us after four or five minutes of precious rest to rise painfully to our feet, help each other on with our packs, and set out again for another kilometer or so on the long road.

It is also a routine that ends each rest break with Harvey's fatherly admonition to me: "Okay, Sonny, let's take our time now," as he sets off at near breakneck speed, leaving me struggling manfully to keep from falling too far behind. It is a constant source of amusement for me to watch Harvey as, eyes straight ahead, he strides along, only to realize when he come to his senses that I have fallen some distance back and he must stop and wait for me. Invariably he apologizes for being in such a hurry and as he gallops away repeats again his favorite instruction for proper hiking: "Okay, Sonny, let's take our time."

Having walked across Newfoundland with Harvey Rice, I think it is safe to say that nobody has watched his rear end more than I.

At five o'clock, with me bringing up the rear as usual, we discover a delightful campsite in a roadside clearing a short distance from a small brook tumbling playfully over a jumble of smooth, black rocks. Here we set up the tent, spread our sleeping bags, tent pads, and clothing atop nearby bushes to catch the late afternoon breeze, and take an invigorating bath in a shady pool formed where the brook pauses briefly in a thick mass of alders.

After supper tonight we relax for some time outside the tent, enjoying the cool of the evening and watching the antics of three young caribou who seem intent on getting past us but are obviously somewhat nervous about our presence. Only after several cautious forays into our private space do they gather sufficient courage to stampede by with a wild kicking of hooves and spraying of rocks. Once safely past, they stop and like young children stare with wide-eyed curiosity at the two strange figures sprawled on the ground.

DAY 15

This morning as we leave camp to hike the remaining twenty-two kilometers to Ebbegumbeag Dam the heavy dew that had settled overnight is fast disappearing under the heat of the late July sun.

Apart from occasional views of the vast expanse of the Maelpaeg Reservoir stretching to the horizon in the southwest and brief glimpses of Island Pond and Crooked Lake to the northeast, today is once again an uneventful, monotonous plodding along a remote, rarely-used stretch of gravel road. Scattered caribou fleeing in momentary shock and numerous spruce grouse fluttering panic-stricken from the bushes do provide some distraction from the punishing heat as we move slowly toward the day's destination in the extreme southeast corner of our current map.

For much of the day our line of travel is almost directly south as the meandering road takes us along the northeastern extremity of the Maelpaeg Reservoir. Gradually the roadside scenery changes. The trees become more scattered, and the country begins to open up, providing at least a more interesting view than yesterday and the first part of today.

For a variety of reasons both Harvey and I find this to be an unusually difficult day. It is now Day 15, and we have not yet taken a break other than the early afternoon conclusion to the rainy Day 10 back at Granite Dyke. For the past five days we have been walking on hard rocky roads with little of scenic interest and without the challenge of route finding or map and compass work. And, of course, there is the knowledge that we are still less than halfway to Sunnyside. These factors naturally take a mental as well as physical toll.

But when we stepped out of the water of St. George's Bay two weeks ago and took our first steps to the east we knew there would be days like this. These, we knew, would be the days that would truly test our mettle and our determination to see this thing through, not the pleasant hikes through beautiful pastoral countryside such as we had experienced beyond Sandy Pond and along the north side of Princess Lake.

The despondency of today ends quickly, however, on our arrival at the Dam around five o'clock. Compared to what we have been used to of late, this is a busy place. The group of trouters from Little Hearts Ease whom we had met yesterday at Noel Paul's Brook have set up an elaborate camp with a huge windbreak for protection against a

Careful footwork required crossing a stream.

southeast wind. At the center of the site is a large camp-fire, and strewn around it are boxes and bags of food and coolers filled with pop, beer, and freshly caught fish. At the opposite end of the clearing three men from Grand Falls-Windsor have set up their truck camper as the base from which to conduct a weekend of fishing, drinking, eating, and simply "getting away from the wife and kids for awhile."

Before even bothering to set up our tent, we drop in on the Little Hearts Ease contingent. Generously they ply us with roasted wieners, left-over pork chops, bread, cookies, and pop, all of which are gourmet items to two hikers who seem to be constantly craving something different and more substantial than the usual fare with which we must content ourselves. Later in the evening the truck campers offer us cold Pepsi and more cookies, and even invite us to share a jiggs dinner which they are preparing for later in the night.

While waiting, we spend some time seriously considering the route we will take on leaving Ebbegumbeag Dam tomorrow. Our map, old and outdated, does not provide enough information as to roads on the eastern side of the dam, and from our vantage point near the edge of the canal through which a torrent of white water spews from the sluice gates, all we can see is a dark green mass of apparently impenetrable forest.

To satisfy our curiosity, we cross the dam just before dark and follow a road which, unmarked on the map, we hope will take us across a low, thickly forested ridge and to a narrow inlet that juts several kilometers inland from the reservoir. We need to find a crossing that will allow us to avoid a long detour. After following this winding road for a kilometer or so and unable to determine exactly in which direction it leads, we head back to our tent. By now darkness is setting in, the wind has increased with a hint of cold rain riding upon it, and we are tired. Too tired in fact to wait up for the enormous pot of salt beef and vegetables steaming on the Coleman stove just across the way. It is a relief to crawl inside our warm sleeping bags. Before long, despite the wind and the incessant roar of rushing water in the canal alongside, we have both drifted off to sleep.

XI. Beyond Ebbegumbeag

Day 16

The easterly wind that began to build last night has arrived with a vengeance and a cold rain is falling when we crawl stiffly out of the tent at 6:15 this morning. Too uncomfortable even to prepare breakfast, we stash our gear, pack the heavy wet tent, and set off across the high concrete dam. A lone trouter shivering on the rocks below looks up and waves. His buddies, after a night of revelry, are still sound asleep. Lucky guys!

Once on the other side of the dam we pick up the gravel road we had followed last night. It takes us about two kilometers along the base of the forested ridge and there before us is a happy circumstance: the road continues across the narrow inlet and deposits us easily and safely at the bottom of the next ridge.

But there the happiness ends. The high, broad ridge before us now is disheartenly green. Our map promises that everything south of where we stand is pleasantly white. Instead we are faced with a wall of mature trees growing out of a floor strewn with enormous boulders and a tangle of fallen deadwood. Another instance where the map cannot be trusted!

By now I am soaked to the skin. Rain drips off my soddened hat and courses down my back like icy fingers. It seeps inside my thin rainpants and traces a cold path down my legs and into my hiking boots. Huge droplets splash onto my eyeglasses, magnifying and distorting the world around me.

The fog has fallen like a wet blanket, wrapping us in an eerie world of mystery and silence. Fighting discomfort, fog and dead trees we follow a compass course to a small pond, no more than two hundred meters in length, on the eastern side of the ridge about three kilometers away. We are now in a thickly-wooded valley that runs southwest for about two kilometers.

Somewhere in this valley, chilled to the bone, we stand beneath the rain-blackened trees and gulp our late breakfast. The day has barely begun and already we seriously discuss whether we should find a place to set up the tent and crawl into warm, dry sleeping bags.

But suddenly, without warning, the wind changes direction. It is a gentle southerly wind that caresses the skin and warms the blood. It shoos away the angry clouds that had been lurking just above the treetops and quickly drives the fog out of the valley.

Our discomfort dissipates as quickly as the clouds and fog. With spirits buoyed on a warm breeze and a hot sun, we continue through the valley, cross a small brook, and begin the long, gradual climb up the base of the ridge whose apex is the prominent Ebbegumbeag Hill.

We are now climbing into open country, and with each contour the view becomes more panoramic and more spectacular. Soon, with the high peak of Ebbegumbeag Hill directly south of us, we are able to drop our packs, sit on a rock, and study the surrounding countryside. To the east is the ocean-like expanse of Meelpaeg, Great Burnt Lake lies partially hidden behind a wooded ridge to the northeast, and to the southeast is the beautiful Cold Spring Pond which is our destination tomorrow.

Under a hot afternoon sun and facing a strong southerly wind, today we head down the ridge, cross a brook that flows northeast into the upper part of Cold Spring Pond, and follow a well-worn caribou trail to a tiny pond set in the bog at the base of the next ridge. It is now four thirty in the afternoon, and considering the conditions we battled this morning, it has been a long day.

On a dry knob about fifty meters from the edge of the pond we set up camp. There we spread all our earthly possessions out to dry on nearby rocks, prepare an early supper, and spend the remainder of the evening just 'lazin around.'

DAY 17

Under a bright morning sun and a cool northerly breeze we leave camp at seven o'clock this morning and head south, following a clear path to the top of a broad, low ridge. The descent of its south side takes us through dense forest with here and there small patches of 'floating bogs' where one misstep could send a pack-laden hiker to the waist in black mud. While negotiating around the edge of one such bog Harvey slips and falls heavily upon his hiking pole, bending it nearly at right angles. His dismay at the possible loss of what has by now become an almost indispensable companion lasts only until he successfully has placed the pole across his leg and coaxed it gently back to its proper shape.

Our concern as we head south today is what appears from the map to be a fairly wide river flowing from a large lake about seven or eight kilometers long into the southern end of Cold Spring Pond. Judging from the enormous watershed feeding into this unnamed lake, we fear the river might be difficult to cross. And if that were the case we would really be in hot water!

But emerging from a band of tuck and following a caribou path through a thin line of conifers, we step onto the rocks at the 'broad river.' It is broad, alright, but certainly not a river—at least not at the moment. Numerous rocks, large and small, provide easy stepping stones to the other side.

Enjoying a sense of relief that another potential obstacle has evaporated, Harvey and I relax for some time on a large rock near the shore. Harvey greedily gulps great quantities of the clear water, while I remove my hat and glasses, bend forward with knees on a rock and hands in the water to take genteel sips of the refreshing liquid.

After taking a few pictures and having a lunch in this beautiful wilderness setting, we head off, invigorated now, to climb a huge barren, rocky ridge that will take us to the extreme south end of Cold Spring Pond. The remainder of the afternoon as we cross the ridge, ford yet another small brook in yet another valley, and walk northeast for about six kilometers atop a magnificent grassy ridge to descend to a gravel road extending from West Salmon Dam, becomes another time of pleasant hiking. The view from those open ridges is spectacular. The glistening surface of Cold Spring Pond stretches far to the north. To the south, just like back at Spruce Pond several days ago, untouched wilderness country blends into a tapestry of green ridges, tan-colored bogs, and dark blotches of forest or tuck. In the east, not far away now, lies the West Salmon hydro development site. We can see the electrical power plant, the neat grey line of the dam itself, and the symmetrical man-made canal running eastward about three kilometers to the Godaleich Generating Station.

At five o'clock, after stumbling through a broad swath of shoulder-high tuck (no caribou trail this time), we break out on a quiet, scenic spot near the edge of the pond. The shoreline, created when the dam forced Cold Spring Pond to invade low-lying areas, appears artificial, with numerous skeletons of drowned trees, creating a dangerous underwater tangle, protruding awkwardly above the calm surface.

But it has been a long and strenuous day, and the surreal silence of tonight's campsite brings it to a relaxing end.

Passing Ebbegumbeag Hill en route to Cold Spring Pond.

XII. On To Bay d'Espoir

Day 18

Today, the first of August, is cloudy at first with an apparent threat of rain. But by the time we leave our camp-site at the far western end of West Salmon Dam to begin the long road hike to Bay d'Espoir, the clouds have disappeared and a refreshing southerly breeze is blowing off the ridges to our right. Great hiking weather.

A short walk sees us at the dam structure itself. I am especially intrigued by the neatness of both the dam and its immediate surroundings. What a contrast to the ugliness of the Granite system further west! The kilometer-long dam and the three kilometer road that follows the edge of the canal to the Godaleich Generating Station are straight and level with an excellent walking surface. On our right, at the base of the dam and canal, we can see a network of tidy access roads leading to various monitoring stations and neat piles of gravel. From the eastern end of the canal to the generating station a triangularly shaped mound of gravel runs straight and true for three or four hundred meters, disappearing into the base of a huge, grey concrete structure at the edge of a deep valley leading into Godaleich Pond about a kilometer to the southeast. Buried beneath the mound, out of sight, we guess, are the enormous pipes through which the waters of Cold Spring Pond and its drainage system flow into the Bay d'Espoir hydro grid and eventually into the homes of St. John's residents as electricity.

But as of yet it is water. And water contains fish. This reservoir, in particular, has a reputation for yielding many fish, huge fish. Harvey is convinced he can catch one here:

guaranteed. So despite my obvious preference to moving on, about halfway across the dam Harvey brings our hike to a momentary hiatus so that he can hook our next meal. For the next half an hour or so, while I relieve my boredom by tossing some of the millions of excellent throwing rocks aimlessly into the reservoir, Harvey passes once again through what has become for him the 'frustrating fishing fiasco.' First there is the Fumbling Through Pack routine to find the reel. Then there is the process of attaching the reel to the telescopic rod, a process for which, at least to my casually watching eye, Harvey's mechanical ability appears woefully inadequate. That finally done, and Harvey already muttering angrily to himself, he clumsily fastens a fly to the hook, a procedure which in my opinion requires the dexterity of a neurosurgeon's hands—dexterity which Harvey's do not have.

Eventually he is ready for the first cast. After several tries he hooks what he excitedly claims is a 'big one,' but it gets away. I find this news disheartening, not because whatever he had hooked got away but because he had hooked something in the first place. Having no pretensions of being a fisherman myself, I get extremely bored watching someone else tossing a line. This hint of success, I am convinced, will only be encouragement for Harvey to keep trying, and already my rock-tossing has created a huge hole in the surface of the dam.

He does keep trying, getting angrier and angrier with each ineffectual toss and tossing harder and harder, trying to reach the opposite side of the reservoir, a kilometer away. Soon the inevitable happens. A vigorous cast causes the reel to dislodge from the rod and follow the hook to a secure hiding place among the rocks near the water's edge, at the bottom of the dam's slippery slope. Repeating words that I can understand only by their tone, Harvey clambers down the rocky incline and retrieves the scattered remains of the reel. I suggest we give up and move on. Several unsuccessful attempts to reconstruct the reel convinces Harvey that maybe we should.

For the remainder of the morning as we leave the West Salmon Dam site behind and head southward towards the bridge that crosses West Salmon River. I have trouble keeping up with Harvey.

By eleven o'clock we are at the bridge. A large sign proclaims this to be the spot beyond which unauthorized vehicles cannot pass because the area encompasses caribou calving grounds. Here during lunch we chat briefly with a Hydro employee and his passenger, well-known radio personality Larry Hudson.

During the day we are fortunate to meet and make the acquaintance of two other Hydro employees. One, Matthew Collier of St. Albans, promises to return during his day off tomorrow with some goodies. Our special requests for Pepsi and Harvey's favorite, sweet biscuits. The other, Ray Buffett, also of St. Albans, chats with us for awhile about our trip and about mutual acquaintances. He gives us the location of his home and offers us the use of his home phone once we reach St. Albans a day or so from now. Thanking him, and once again impressed by the friendliness and generosity of the people we meet along the way, we continue the long road south to St. Albans-Bay d'Espoir.

Tonight, after hiking a distance of twenty-seven kilometers, we camp on a high bluff near a small, clear brook that runs into the northeast end of Ahwachanjeesh Pond, a pond whose name is as difficult to say as it is to spell.

Supper, a bath, an hour or so of relaxation, and the pleasant feeling of having met new friends provide the perfect antidote for tired bodies and the day's early frustrations.

DAY 19

When we get up at ten minutes before six this morning the sun is rising brilliantly above the barren ridge to the east. But upon leaving camp two hours later the sky has already clouded over and rain seems imminent.

Rain does indeed begin shortly after we start walking. It is a bone-chilling drizzle, accompanied by a cold northerly wind. We thought the weather conditions that day back at Granite Lake when we were able to seek shelter in the camp near Granite Dyke to be bad and we believed the cold rain that chilled us so deeply upon leaving Ebbegumbeag Dam was punishing, but this is worse. This lasts all day with no hint that it will ever end.

With the northerly wind biting into our backs, cutting through our soggy rainclothes, and the cold rain running down our necks, we plod determinedly along, inching our way southward, taking only scattered brief, unpleasant rests. The land is featureless today as the gravel road winds through forest, avoiding bogs and open country and staying a little distant from the shores of ponds and lakes. Throughout the day we judge our location by small brooks that cross the road, ridges that must be climbed, and occasional glimpses of large bodies of water.

If not for people we meet, the day would be a masterpiece of monotony. Matthew Collier, true to his word, arrives from St. Albans, his small son asleep at his side, and delivers a litre of Pepsi—on ice!— and a package of sweet biscuits. Before leaving, he provides details as to where we can find a suitable campsite later in the evening. Ray Buffett, returning to St. Albans from his work back near the Dam, gives us a liter of orange juice. Peter Hewlett, from our hometown of Springdale, on his way home from a line-cutting project north of the West Salmon Dam area, stops to share mutual surprise at us meeting him and him meeting us. We chat briefly. From the warm, dry confines of his pickup, he informs us that he and his buddy have quit work early because the weather is so miserable–'not fit for working outdoors.'

Certainly no consolation for the two desolate wretches he leaves behind as he pulls away. Tired, wet, and cold, we drop down into the deep gorge of Salmon River, which flows to the southwest out of Jeddore Lake, cross a high steel bridge, and begin the long climb up the side of a broad ridge that is forested on the north but barren and flat at the top. Crossing the bridge, we look down at the remains of what once must have been a proud river. Now, thanks to a dam built a kilometer upstream where it empties out of Jeddore Lake, it has been reduced to little more than an ineffectual trickle.

About halfway up the ridge we stop at the gravel pit campsite Matthew Collier had told us about, eat a hasty supper, and without further ado crawl into our warm, dry sleeping bags. It is barely past six o'clock, but after twenty-eight long kilometers and ten miserable hours of walking, this day ends not a moment too soon.

DAY 20

The community of Head of Bay d'Espoir is still more than eighteen kilometers away when we leave camp under a cloudless sky to hike along the south side of Jeddore Lake as far as Camp Boggy, a Hydro workers camp just south of the Bay d'Espoir Generating Station.

The walk, pleasant in the hot sun after yesterday's misery, is uneventful. Seeing sections of the vast expanse of Jeddore Lake, crossing South Dam, passing the Bay d'Espoir Airfield, and exchanging brief pleasantries with a bearded man in a small, dilapidated car, prove to be the only diversions this morning.

After a noon lunch on a brook near Camp Boggy, where I spill the entire contents of a freeze-dried meal proving once again that I am, as Harvey loves to proclaim, a 'real ninny,' we walk the remaining distance to the Bay d'Espoir Motel on a paved highway. There we spend the remainder of the afternoon and evening eating, showering, washing clothes, watching television, and phoning home. In my case, the phone call home has special significance, this being August 3rd and therefore the anniversary of the beginning of my married life. In 1993 the trek from south to north had prevented my wife Gleason and me from being together on our twenty-fifth. Now the attempt to walk from west to east is keeping us apart on the twenty-seventh. Not to worry, Bert, she reminds me, the celebration doesn't have to be on August 3rd!

Ensconced on soft mattresses, clean and well-rested, we take stock. Twenty days have gone by since St. George's Bay, and 385 unbroken kilometers have passed beneath our feet. We have walked through all kinds of weather and have lugged our packs over every conceivable type of Newfoundland terrain. We have met interesting people, increased our store of memories, and learned valuable lessons about our physical and mental limitations.

Those limitations, we realize, could now be the key to success. By our guess another ten or eleven days remain. Already we have been hiking one day longer than we have ever hiked before. Can our bodies endure another eleven days? Can we handle the constant mental strain that comes from having no other company but each other's, of walking endlessly day after day, and from the repeated packing and unpacking of backpacks and ritual setting up and dismantling of the tent?

The answers to those questions lie ahead.

XIII. To Jipujijkuei And Beyond

Day 21

Today from start to finish is sunny and hot. For Harvey and me it is a trying stretch of walking for eighteen or so kilometers to Jipujijkuei Provincial Park where the plan is for us to meet Jim Huxter and take on our final food supply before heading east to Sunnyside.

Beyond the junction to Milltown, the road takes us northeast for ten long kilometers before connecting with the Harbour Breton Road and looping back to the south. A short distance south on the Harbour Breton Road we cross the bridge spanning Conne River. It being one thirty in the afternoon and our feet burning from the constant pounding on hot pavement, we stop beneath the bridge to have a lunch and soak our feet in the cold water.

We have just completed a long, arduous climb to the top of a high ridge and are sprawled exhausted against our packs at the side of the road, when Jim, his wife Betty, and Harvey's two daughters, Heather and Jennifer, brake to a stop a few meters away. Once excited greetings are dispensed with—Harvey's fatherly slobbering over his girls being especially maudlin—we pile into Jim's Mazda MPV and drive the short distance to Jipujijkuei Park. There Harvey and I are courted with homemade bread, muffins, corned beef, and ice cold Pepsi.

At 4:30, socializing over, we are again dropped off at the spot where we were picked up, good-byes are said, and we set off carrying a ten-day supply into the bush. A short distance along the transmission line, we find a little dry spot among the alders near a tiny brook and set up for the night.

We can't wait for tomorrow. From here on we anticipate good hiking, much better than what we have experienced so far. Just goes to show how naive even seasoned hikers can be.

DAY 22

This morning, already sweating profusely in the warm, humid conditions, we begin the long slog eastward. For the next forty or so kilometers the terrain is mostly heavily forested with scattered sections of wet bog. Fortunately the transmission line that runs in a relatively straight line from the Bay d'Espoir Generating Station all the way to St. John's is right on our route. Our plan is to follow this line as far as Hungry Grove Pond, at which point the country opens up and we will be able to take whatever path we please.

For the present, we are confined to the line. And it is a good thing, too. A wall of seemingly impenetrable forest—the kind that has tall, thin trees growing only inches apart—stretches endlessly on both sides of the cut line. There is no way, we tell each other, that a loaded backpacker can maneuver through this stuff.

To our chagrin, right from the outset the going is rough—as rough as anything we have faced so far. An endless series of ridges, running north to south, lie across the route. Up these ridges we tote our sixty-plus pound packs, legs screaming in agony and hearts pounding feverishly. Then in the valleys we navigate spongy, wet bogs churned soft and black by heavy Hydro machinery that had travelled the line before us.

Six difficult kilometers puts us at the edge of Little River. This river, flowing southeast, is fed by the waters of Koskaecodde Lake and Jubilee Lake and empties into Bay d'Espoir. It is not a huge river, but at this point it is narrow and fast. We stop to remove our boots, socks, and trousers and, with packs unbuckled, wade across to the other side.

Shortly after noon we enter the Bay du Nord Wilderness Reserve, its boundary marked only by a bullet-scarred sign warning against hunting and ATV use. This being an area set aside as a preserve, entry requires a permit. For reassurance, I ask Harvey if he still has ours. He does.

Two kilometers beyond the reserve boundary we arrive at the Bay du Nord River. Here, at the point where the river flows out of the enormous body of water known as Medonnegonix Lake, Hydro has recently constructed a bridge. Lucky for us. A quick check of the river shows that for some unknown reason it is much higher than normal. Grass and low bushes that had grown along the river's edge during the summer are now submerged beneath the water.

In a clearing on a high bank a short distance back from the water's edge is a sturdily constructed Hydro building, its windows and doors tightly barred. No chance of finding refuge in this fortress. Near the building a wooden platform measuring approximately twenty-five square meters has been built as a helicopter landing pad. Realizing that a good tent site will be virtually impossible to find if we push on and that we are already exhausted, the landing pad becomes our tent pad. We set up, though it is not yet late in the evening, and enjoy an early supper.

Fairness demands that, considering my report on Harvey's fishing fiasco back at West Salmon Dam, I admit to some success on his part this evening. Following supper he tosses his line into the fabled water of Medonnegonix Lake, the lake where giant fish abound, where professional fishermen, local and foreign, pay big dollars to toss theirs. Lo and behold, Harvey lands an eight-inch ouaniniche. A fine meal it would make. But we have just finished supper. Following a brief discussion about the pros and cons of hanging on to this fine piscine specimen, the decision is made to return it to the lake. The lucky ouaniniche pauses beneath a rock to recover from momentary disorientation, and swims away forever thankful for 'hook and release' fishermen.

Drinking water from Bay du Nord River.

XIV. OUT OF THE BAY DU NORD WILDERNESS

DAY 23

At seven-thirty this morning, well-rested and basking in occasional periods of hot sun, we cross the Hydro bridge spanning the Bay du Nord River and continue our eastward journey. It soon becomes clear that travelling conditions are not about to improve. The ridges seem steeper, the bogs wider and softer. Most of the boggy sections, in fact, seem nothing more than carpets of tufted grass floating on a bottomless pit of oozing black mud. As we hop across those, our hiking poles prove to be indispensable. They become probes with which to judge firmness of foot placements and stabilizers when it is necessary to hang precariously onto branches while skirting around especially deep bogholes.

Struggling along in this manner we soon leave Medonnegonix Lake behind and angle slightly southeast to cross a long, tree-covered esker, or low ridge of sand, that runs from the west side of an unnamed pond about six kilometers to the south and ends as a point of land jutting into the southern end of Koskaecodde Lake. From there a short jaunt takes us to the beginning of a long detour through the forest at the south end of a huge, shallow pond, a detour that besides taking us around the pond also leads us out of the Bay du Nord Wilderness.

Now that the Reserve is behind me I can look back at it and evaluate my impressions. I had expected this area to be filled with scenic beauty and teeming with wildlife. Neither was the case. Thick forests, hidden ponds, and squishy bogs never were my idea of natural beauty. As for wildlife, there was some, but not in the abundance I expected. We did spot several loons in flight, a fox, an enormous moose, and a few caribou—including four lying on a dry section of bog. And Harvey did manage to hook a ouaniniche. My feeling is that the Bay du Nord Wilderness Reserve may indeed be a hunter's and fisherman's—perhaps even a canoeist's—paradise. But for the backpacker, at least in the section through which we travelled, it has little to offer.

For the remainder of the day the terrain gradually changes. Bogs are more widely scattered and less wet, and the forest begins to thin out. The improved conditions make progress easier, and by late afternoon we have reached a lovely little brook at the base of a ridge just west of Hungry Grove Pond. It being this late and Harvey's left knee beginning to weaken, we choose a spot on the grassy bank near the brook and set up camp. Despite the prospect of much better travelling country from this point on, Harvey's problem knee causes a little concern tonight.

XV. LONG HARBOUR RIVER

DAY 24

A cool northerly breeze and good walking allow us to cover great distance this morning. It is still early in the day when we pass through the final stretch of forest, at the north end of Hungry Grove Pond, and enjoy the gratifying sight of trees first becoming more dispersed and then disappearing altogether. Now a broad vista of barren, open country spreads before us. After three days confined within the prison of thick growth, the view is exhilarating.

By one o'clock we have reached Kanes Brook, the first of a series of beautiful streams that flow from the north, carving meandering valleys, sinuous lines of green drawn on an otherwise barren landscape. Removing our boots and socks, as we'd had to do earlier to cross a brook flowing uncharacteristically north from Hungry Grove Pond, we wade across Kanes Brook and lunch on the opposite bank.

The remainder of the afternoon is one of those times of pleasurable hiking. The weather is neither too hot nor too cold, mosquitoes are virtually non-existent, and caribou sightings have become routine. The ground is hard and dry, and we can set a steady pace, enjoying the marvelous views that seem to get even more spectacular with each ridge we cross. The emphasis now is as much on taking pictures as it is on walking.

Maintaining this relaxed pace, mid-afternoon finds us at Beaver Brook, our campsite for tonight.

Beaver Brook is a stream that flows southward, originating in ponds far to the north near Mount Sylvester and gaining size as it collects water from numerous tributaries draining the bogs of Eastern Maelpaeg. Four kilometers to the south of our campsite the brook merges with Long Harbour River, from where the two converge into one to empty into Fortune Bay. Today Beaver Brook is wide, shallow, and rocky, very similar in physical characteristics to White Bear River, though infinitely more beautiful.

We set up our tent in deep grass on the western bank, the door facing the river. With sleeping pads and bags spread out to air in the warm sun of early evening, Harvey and I change into sandals and go to separate sections of the river for an evening bath. He walks downstream, and I stroll along the grassy bank upstream, around a bend. There I strip for a vigorous, refreshing bath, wash several garments, and using my compass mirror and a Bic razor, scrape twenty-three days' growth off my face.

After supper a sudden torrential downpour forces us to seek shelter in the tent. The cloudburst is brief, and on its passing leaves in its wake a beautiful double rainbow, a

Cleanup time. Shaving with the aid of a compass mirror, after a bath in a nearby stream.

brilliant spectrum of color glowing with promise in the eastern sky.

With this omen of a bright tomorrow, our spirits are buoyant tonight. Tomorrow will be day twenty-five, and the chances of reaching Sunnyside in another six or seven days are looking better all the time. Harvey's knee, since he has taken to wearing a brace, is holding up well. The hiking is superb and will apparently continue to be so. Our packs are getting lighter every day. And the fresh bear tracks we saw in the mud earlier today are now a long reassuring distance away.

Crossing Long Harbour River.

DAY 25

Early this morning, only four kilometers into the day, we arrive at the Long Harbour River. With its reputation as one of the island's significant rivers, this is another whose crossing we had feared because of what we thought might be inadequate information about its depth and strength of current. We had been told by Hydro people at Whitbourne that near the transmission line it would be wide and shallow. Would it be?

Happily, it is both. Unlike the swollen Bay du Nord River, water levels here are extremely low. Here, where the land is flat and the river bends to the west, it is rocky and broad, much wider than any of the rivers we have crossed so far. Choosing our route from rock to rock, we once again remove boots and trousers and cross easily to the other side. From this point on we know that no river, at least, will hold us back. North Harbour River and Come By Chance River still lie across our path, but having checked them out last summer, we know they will pose no problems.

As the verdant valley through which flows Long Harbour River fades in the distance behind us, the terrain becomes harder and the walking even easier. We are no longer restricted to the transmission line but are instead free to follow whatever route we wish so long as it is in an easterly direction and keeps us away from large bodies of water. We are now on the Gisborne Lake topographical map, a map that is almost entirely white, speckled with thousands of tiny blue ponds and waterholes. A fearsome thirty kilometer wide bog, if one were to give the map a casual glance. But no. In reality we have struck upon ideal hiking country.

And the view is breathtaking. Staying north of the transmission line and sticking to the high country, we watch as magnificent scenes leap from the landscape onto our rolls of Kodak. Spectacular views of prominent landmarks such as Pin Hill, a high knob to the north, as well as Dunns Mountain, Dunns Mountain Pond, Carole's Hat, and Nine Mile Hill to the south simply cry out to be photographed. And photograph them we do!

The day passes quickly. At four-thirty we set up camp on a small knoll directly above Dunn's Brook with Pin Hill looming on one hand and Dunns Mountain standing distant, barren, and aloof on the other. It is a picturesque campsite, a far cry from the one back at Princess Lake where we'd had to wedge the tent between two trees in a thick, wet forest.

Tonight as a giant moon brightens the tent and fills the barrens with a ghostly light, the darkest shadows are caused by strange restless cries from geese to the north, and by Harvey's sore throat with what seems to be a touch of the flu.

On the Swift Current Barrens. Dunn's Mountain in the background.

XVI. CROSSING THE SWIFT CURRENT BARRENS

DAY 26

Stifling heat exacerbated by a hot wind saps our energy today as we hike the seventeen kilometers from Dunn's Brook to Wigman Brook, a lovely stream that flows out of Otter Pond to the north and connects with Sandy Harbour River just below the magnificent, barren Sandy Harbour Ridge.

We are now crossing the starkly beautiful Swift Current Barrens. Caribou are in abundance here, moving slowly in groups of up to a dozen, apparently more curious than afraid at our intrusion. Geese, too, are plentiful. They rise majestically from numerous ponds as we appear and, with deep-throated honks and a great flapping of wings, fly in formation to other ponds close by but just out of sight.

The surrounding beauty is what keeps us going today. Harvey's sore throat of last night has worsened and he is suffering from unmistakable symptoms of the flu. Popping lozenges and gulping down large quantities of water at every stream provide him with some relief from the throat problem, but it is no answer for the illness that he says saps energy from every muscle in his body. I too am finding the effects today of a fatigue that has gradually been building since leaving Robinsons twenty-five days ago.

It seems to be finally catching up with us. The constant walking, day in and day out, without a prolonged break; the struggling through what at times has been rough terrain with a heavy load on our back; the routine of fumbling through a pack for every item, no matter how insignificant; and the monotony of the same diet for weeks on end have all begun to take a heavy toll.

Travelling in this mood, we leave Dunn's Brook and for nearly a kilometer head almost directly north to avoid a large boggy area that lies across our route. From there our course, though generally eastward, traces a meandering line around dozens of ponds, some large, most little more than natural swimming holes.

Fortunately, the terrain here is excellent for walking. The barrens are hard, mostly covered with yellowed grass or low, ground-hugging shrubs. Some spots, totally devoid of vegetation, are merely patches of hard gravel. In other places, where once there had been bog are now stretches of black mud, cracked and baked hard in the August sun. Thankful for such good going, we plod steadily on through the sweltering heat of the day.

Despite the almost mind numbing monotony of the routine and the insipid effect of fatigue, we are still able to appreciate the beauty of our surroundings. The vastness and openness of these barrens, and the teeming wildlife, especially geese and caribou, still elicit their usual thrill, prompting us over and over again to drop our packs, search for our cameras, and try vainly to capture the magnificence of the scenery.

One feature in particular catches our attention and holds it throughout today. It is the geological feature known as the Tolt that juts out of the otherwise rolling landscape about ten or eleven kilometers to the north. Despite the connotation of ugliness the comparison suggests, the prominence of the Tolt on the smooth surface of the barrens is somewhat similar to the effect of a wart on the skin of a beautiful woman. It, and not the surroundings, is what draws our attention.

Late in the afternoon we reach Wigman's Brook. Like all of the brooks we have encountered since crossing Bay du Nord River several days ago, this one is shallow and rocky as well. Crossing on the rocks, we discover a large clearing only a couple of hundred meters back from the river. There we set up camp again, a procedure that by now has become automatic, and lug our gear down to the river's edge to wash up and prepare supper.

Harvey does not eat well this evening. Partly thankful because it means I can have more than my usual share, but mostly concerned because Sunnyside is still at least four long walking days away, I try to encourage him to eat all of his freeze-dried meal. Instead he tosses much of it into the river. For some time we sit on the rocks, not speaking much, staring at the water, watching it busily negotiate its way to the south. When we do speak, it is to comment on our exhaustion, on the fact that we couldn't have gone any farther today, that we have reached our limit. I feel sorry for Harvey at this point because I know that with his sore throat, which has worsened, and the effects of his flu, he must be finding it even more difficult than I.

Suddenly, we are jolted from our listlessness. The unmistakable sound of an all-terrain vehicle has broken the silence. Before we even get a chance to scramble to our feet, an ATV sputters to a stop at the water's edge and a young fellow whom I judge to be perhaps in his twenties, visibly surprised to encounter two miserable looking wretches sprawled among the rocks in this remote place, tosses a greeting to us. Energized now, we tell him who we are, what we are doing, and why—at least we try to explain why: who knows why anyone would do this anyway?

The young man, pleasant and friendly, introduces himself as Dedreic Grecian, a Memorial University biology student who, as a summer project, is studying the geese population on the Swift Current Barrens. He is on his way to his camp on Dunn's Brook to pick up his personal belongings and plans to return to Swift Current tomorrow.

We chat for some time, sharing experiences. After several broad hints thrown his way by Harvey, Dedreic also shares some of his food. Suddenly Harvey can eat again. Sensing our desperation for something different in the culinary field, Dedreic also promises that tomorrow, on his return, he will cook a jiggs dinner for us. Thanking him but not staking our lives on that actually happening, we part. His ATV splashes across the river, bounces up the embankment on the opposite side and disappears into the gathering darkness. We wash our dishes, collect our gear, and retreat to the tent.

We are feeling much better now. A beautiful moon lights up the countryside, inquisitive caribou loiter around our tent, and the cries of loons and geese fill the night as we drift off to sleep.

DAY 27

Again today the earth bakes under a clear blue sky. In the morning we leave our campsite at Wigman Brook to hike the remaining fifteen kilometers to the Burin Peninsula Highway. The walking conditions are similar to what they have been for the past two or three days now. Even the several huge bogs that we have to cross, although churned up by ATV's, are hard and provide good walking.

The prospect of extra goodies and perhaps even a jiggs dinner later this evening plus the knowledge that the highway is getting closer with each step spurs us on. We travel steadily, maintaining a rapid pace. At noon we lunch near a tiny brook. One final low ridge lies between us and the road.

It is still only two o'clock in the afternoon when we wade across another small brook and enter a large clearing. From here a gravel road leads to the highway. While Harvey sits and guards our packs I stroll a kilometer or so out the road to the edge of a large pond to see whether a better campsite is available. A sandy beach strewn with garbage and scattered piles of ashes from previous beach parties does not entice. Content with what we have, we select a grassy spot at the edge of the clearing and set up the tent.

No sooner is that chore completed than our new friend Dedreic appears, his ATV piled high with camping paraphernalia and, we hope, food. Sure enough, while Harvey and I lounge luxuriously, he graciously plies us with Pepsi, bars, cookies, and whatever other tidbits of food he can find in his larder. Throughout the afternoon as he busily prepares vegetables and salt beef for what we anticipate will be a sumptuous evening meal, we enjoy each others' company. Harvey and I, when pressed, tell him about our previous hiking accomplishments and when further pressed, give him all the details. It takes most of the afternoon.

Darkness has nearly set in when we finish washing the dishes. Sluggish from an afternoon of nibbling on snacks and an eight o'clock feast of jiggs dinner, we bid Dedreic goodbye and retire to our tent.

It has been an interesting day. And tomorrow we will be on pavement.

XVII. On The Burin Peninsula Highway

Day 28

It is Friday, August 11th, another hot day, as we walk the gravel road just over a kilometer to the Burin Peninsula Highway. About 7 kilometers to the east is Pipers Hole River, a spot with an interesting history, and another seven or eight kilometers beyond that is the community of Swift Current. The end is definitely getting near, and already our excitement is beginning to build.

Once again, as had been the case when we hit the Burgeo Highway and later the Bay d'Espoir Highway, we experience the unfamiliar sensation of cars and trucks rushing by, seeming to barely miss us as we walk along the rocky shoulder. It is certainly different from the wilderness hiking with its comforting silence and peacefulness to which we have become accustomed.

Almost without exception, as vehicles pass by we notice that drivers stare into their rear view mirrors and passengers crane their necks for a better look. We must be a strange sight. By now we have both lost considerable weight, and according to my mother I was never much more than 'skin and bones' at the best of times…Harvey is bearded; my face is disfigured by an ugly stubble. We are gaunt, and bent forward beneath the weight of our packs. Our hiking pants, deeply stained with chlorophyll and bog water, are by now much the worse for wear. Harvey's has a long rip in one leg, and mine are sporting a crotch crudely sewn. Our hats, after enduring endless days in all kinds of weather and being treated to every conceivable form of abuse are shapeless and faded, with streaks of rust running from eyelet holes to brim. Top all of that off with an image of us leaning on our hiking poles, and you have a picture of two bedraggled, destitute men hobbling along the side of a highway. No wonder they wanted a clearer view!

We look so destitute, in fact, that at some point in the afternoon a woman driving a late model, full-sized pickup pulls onto the shoulder, leans across, and asks us if we are okay. My initial thought—that she is impressed to see two obviously very tough men carrying such enormous loads and is about to proposition us—is only momentary. Reality can be so harsh.

Around ten o'clock we descend into the deep gully through which Pipers Hole River makes it way to Placentia Bay. We pass the entrance to Pipers Hole Park, a lovely, quiet little provincial park in which Harvey and I camped last summer during one of our exploratory trips. The sign at the park entrance reminds me of a fascinating story written on another, much larger, sign in the park itself. The story goes like this:

> *In the late 17th and early 18th centuries, fishing boats would come to Newfoundland every summer to fish. One particular ship carried a crew of Englishmen and one Scotsman—named Kelly. Kelly loved to play the bagpipes. Often in the evening he would play for the men. On nice evenings many of the men would go ashore to hunt or explore the landscape. The wind was strong on this trip, however one Englishman named Morrissey decided to go ashore and do a little hunting. He persuaded Kelly to accompany him and the two men set off. Accidentally Morrissey shot Kelly. Morrissey started to panic and put Kelly's body and gun into a nearby pond. In the confusion he did not notice the growing storm. It was too stormy to reach the moored ship so he spent three days in a cave before he was able to return. Upon boarding he told the*

crew that somehow he and Kelly had strayed apart. A search was ordered by the captain but Kelly's body was not found. It was assumed he was either killed by Indians or died of exposure.

From that day on the residents of the nearby area heard piping music at dusk. Many years later the music stopped just as mysteriously as it started. The same night the piping music stopped, an old sailor died across the ocean in England. As he lay on his deathbed, he confessed to a young priest the accident which happened many years ago in Newfoundland, by Pipers Hole. Coincidentally, a few years later the priest was stationed in Newfoundland not far from Pipers Hole. The residents told him of the strange story of how the piping music started and stopped without any known reason. The priest remembered the confession of the old sailor and in amazement realized Kelly's ghost was responsible.

An intriguing story of murder and mystery. I am reminded again of similar tales whose ghosts seemed to hover over The Grasses over four hundred kilometers to the west, those stories of Scotsmen struggling to scratch a living from the land and whispered rumours of blood spilling upon the green grass.

The haunting sound of bagpipes has long since died here at Pipers Hole as we pass by. The rush of traffic and noise of construction on the bridge tell us we are now in a place and time where such romantic stories have no appeal. Does the murdered Kelly's ghost still linger in the shadowy gully to the north, I wonder? Could it be that he is still piping, but nobody hears?

Back to the present. The seven kilometer walk from Pipers Hole to Swift Current is pleasurable. This stretch of highway skirts along the north side of a long inlet of Placentia Bay that pokes far inland to the northwest between a series of high mountains brooding on either side. It is a scenic stroll made even more pleasant by a refreshing cool breeze that blows off the bay.

We lunch on chicken with chips and gravy at the Kilmory Resort convenience store near the highway just outside Swift Current. There we take advantage of the public telephone to call home and make arrangements to be picked up by our wives at Sunnyside on Sunday. By late afternoon we are across the Black River Bridge, about five kilometers east of Swift Current, and have set up camp in a clearing among the brush near the side of the highway. There we have a hearty supper of bologna and beans, a couple of luxury items we had managed to pick up at a small, understocked little store back in Swift Current.

As Day 28 ends, our spirits are high. The fatigue of two days ago has disappeared, and we feel ready to conquer the North Harbour Ridge—the last ridge of any significance that lies between us and our destination.

XVIII. THE HOME STRETCH

DAY 29

Today begins with promise of being another scorcher. By eight o'clock when we leave camp after a fine breakfast of fried ham and boiled eggs (minus the butter!) it is already very hot. But by the time we have hiked the couple of kilometers to the gravel road that is to take us from the Burin Peninsula Highway across to the North Harbour Road a dense fog has rolled in, obscuring the sun and sending a chill into our bones.

From the North Harbour Road we follow a muddy ATV trail to the edge of a deep gorge through which flows North Harbour River. Very carefully we lower ourselves and our packs down a sheer drop of about five meters to the river itself. There in the shelter of the small cliff we relax for about half an hour over a snack and cool water before tackling the exhausting climb up the opposite side.

The remainder of the afternoon we spend traversing the ridge between us and the Come By Chance River. The fog is heavy, forcing us to follow the transmission line which cuts a broad swath across the top of the ridge. Once again, as we had been when crossing the ridge between White Bear River and the Granite Lake Road, we are enveloped in an eerie white world of silence. I muse that if the dead Scotsman Kelly should choose to play his pipes here rather than back at Pipers Hole he would surely be heard.

But we hear nothing other than an occasional snipe, irritated at our intrusion, and the slurp of our boots as they are being yanked out of wet bog. The bogs are numerous on this ridge, and they are wet and deep. We had thought that confining ourselves to the power line would make the going easier. But no. It is the Bay du Nord Wilderness all over again.

At 2:30, after a couple of hours picking our way across bogs, following the ghostly outlines of huge poles looming out of the fog, we suddenly begin to descend sharply, and the fog almost as suddenly begins to lift. We have emerged from our last spell of total isolation. Symbolically, the fog rolls back like a veil, revealing the pretty little town of Come By Chance just across the river, the oil refinery a short distance away, and a thin line of pavement running along the top of the next ridge. This, we recognize excitedly, is the Trans Canada Highway. A steady stream of cars, trucks, and RV's, all of dinky toy proportions from this distance, can be seen rushing east and west along the ridge. Do they know they are atop a ridge, I wonder?

Seeing the TCH like this is further confirmation that our long journey is nearly over and our dream is about to be realized. The last time we had seen the TCH was on Day 1 when, shortly after leaving Robinsons, we had left it to begin the long walk on the gravel road leading to Mica Pond and the Grasses. That was many days, many kilometers, and untold footsteps ago.

A few more footsteps, careful ones too, take us down the steep, slippery slope to the edge of the Come By Chance River. We wade across with our boots on and after a short search find a suitable location among the bushes not far from the river. Here we establish our final campsite.

Day 30

We have the luxury of sleeping late this morning. It is only a couple of hours walk from here, through the town of Come By Chance, across the highway, and out the side road to Sunnyside. We don't expect Gleason and Barb to pick us up until lunch time at the earliest, so what's the hurry? That's what Harvey keeps reminding me every time I threaten to get up and go outside. I am impatient to get on the move, but Harvey as usual is quite content to relax for awhile.

At 10 o'clock I have finally convinced him it is time for action. The fog and rain that had persisted throughout the night has by now disappeared and the weather has become hot and humid. We breakfast on cereal and boiled eggs (again no butter) and for the final time take down the tent and pack it away. It is an emotional moment—not to the point of tears, mind you—this dismantling for the last time of what has for the past month been our only home. In fact, every camp chore we undertake this morning is made significant by its finality.

An easy, uneventful hike sees us at 12:30 on Sunday afternoon on the rocky beach of Sunnyside stepping into the water of Trinity Bay. Except for the curious stares of someone looking through the window of a nearby house, we are alone. Our wives have not yet arrived. There is no fanfare; there are no interviewers quizzing us about our feelings now that the end is here; there are no cameras recording the conclusion of this first known crossing of the island from west to east. Like our departure from Robinsons, this is clearly not a significant event as far as John Q. Public is concerned.

But for Harvey and me the formality of deliberately wetting our boots in Trinity Bay is very significant. With the simple act we are ceremoniously washing boots that have created an unbroken line of footprints for 540 kilometers from the shore of St. George's Bay on Newfoundland's west coast to this spot on the east. It is a line of footprints that has scuffed the gravel of numerous woods roads, dented the grass on vast stretches of beautiful Newfoundland barrens, broken spiny twigs off far too many stunted spruce, sunk deep into the black mud of hundreds of bogs, and stirred the bottoms of countless streams.

We have made the dream a reality. And now sprawled on the ground, resting on our packs as we await our wives' arrival, that torturous climb to the craggy ledge above far-away Mica Pond nearly a month ago seems already a distant memory.

Distant, yes. But a memory that will remain. How could we ever forget? How can one forget the experiences that come with backpacking through the unspoiled and ruggedly beautiful wilderness of Newfoundland? Though anxious to meet our wives, whom we have missed, and though already salivating in anticipation of waiting culinary delights, we both agree that as for backpacking, we have not yet had our fill.

Journey's end at Sunnyside, Trinity Bay on Nfld's East Coast, thirty days and 540 kilometers after leaving Robinsons.

Gros Morne
National Park

Gros Morne National Park
Michael Burzynski
ISBN 1-55081-135-5 / $49.95 (hc)
6" x 9" / 240 pp.

Gros Morne National Park is a comprehensive guide to the largest and most spectacular national park in Canada—one of the best known parks yet one of the least visited. It is renown as a **UNESCO** World Heritage Site and for its unexpected landscapes, spectacular plants and abundant wildlife, all of which are described in detail complete with colour photographs throughout. This book reveals both the accessible park and its hidden treasures. It includes information on services, campgrounds, trails and other facilities. This is an indispensible book for planning a trip in any season or as a lasting keepsake.

Forty Testoons

Alan Fisk
ISBN 1-55081-145-2 / $17.95 (sc)
5" x 8" / 224 pp.

This is a novel of political intrigue, spies and treason in medieval Newfoundland. The year is 1504 and Father Ralph Fletcher, a young priest, is paid forty silver coins called testoons to stay and minister to the winter crew while the summer fleet returns to England. He becomes swept up in intrigue, as the winter crew attempts to depose King Henry VII of England in favour of a Yorkist pretender. Father Ralph's role in the plot becomes clear—he is to sanctify the actions, while striving to convert the native Beothuk to Christianity.

All Gone Widdun

Annamarie Beckel
ISBN 1-55081-147-9 / $19.95 (sc)
5" x 8" / 280 pp.

This is a novel of one man's quixotic mission to save the Beothuk of Newfoundland from extinction, his love for Shawnadithit, and the tragedy of her life and the lives of her people. Based on true accounts, the novel is told in the alternating first-person narratives of William Epps Cormack, an eccentric Newfoundland-born Scottish merchant, and Shawnadithit, a young Beothuk woman captured by English settlers in 1823 who proved to be the last Beothuk.

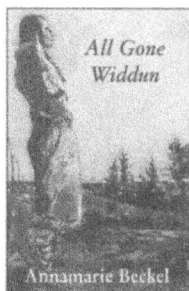

www.ingramcontent.com/pod-product-compliance
Lightning Source LLC
LaVergne TN
LVHW091159080426
835509LV00006B/755